# Southern Living GARDEN GUIDE

# Trees

*Series Editor: Lois Trigg Chaplin*

*Text by Glenn Morris*

OXMOOR
HOUSE®

# Contents

Library of Congress Catalog Number: 95-74604
ISBN: 0-8487-2242-6
Manufactured in the United States of America
First Printing 1996

Editor-in-Chief: Nancy Fitzpatrick Wyatt
Editorial Director, Special Interest Publications:
Ann H. Harvey
Senior Editor, Editorial Services: Olivia Kindig Wells
Art Director: James Boone

*Southern Living* Garden Guide TREES

Series Editor: Lois Trigg Chaplin
Assistant Editor: Kelly Hooper Troiano
Copy Editor: Jennifer K. Mathews
Editorial Assistant: Catherine Barnhart Pewitt
Garden Editor, *Southern Living*: Linda C. Askey
Indexer: Katharine R. Wiencke
Concept Designer: Eleanor Cameron
Designer: Carol Loria
Senior Photographer, *Southern Living*: Van Chaplin
Production and Distribution Director: Phillip Lee
Associate Production and Distribution Manager:
John Charles Gardner
Associate Production Manager: Theresa L. Beste
Production Assistants:
Marianne Jordan Wilson, Valerie Heard

Our appreciation to the staff of *Southern Living*
magazine for their contributions to this book.

*Red cedar*

*Southern magnolia*

Cover (from left): *Blue spruce,
sassafras, magnolia*
Frontispiece: *Redbud*

*Hickory*

# Trees Primer

*Planting a tree is a gift of shade, shelter, and joy to the future. Your choice will be a living tribute for generations.*

*The scarlet blush of oaks comes with cool, sunny weather.*

Perhaps you have looked down the avenue of oaks at Boone Hall Plantation near Charleston or walked through a springtime shower of cherry-blossom petals in Washington, D.C. Who has not discovered a beech tree with initials carved in the bark? If you have visited these historic sites or happened upon other groves, you have witnessed the timeless power of trees.

Trees provide the visual background that frames homes, schools, and other structures of daily life. They subconsciously define nostalgic places; dogwoods may subtly remind you of your childhood home. One tree with exemplary form—a sighing weeping cherry, a formal Bradford pear, or a massive Southern magnolia—is so compelling that the memory of a place is the memory of the tree.

Trees may also define an entire geographic region. The villages of New England owe much of their picturesque quality to the sugar maple, the tree of choice for town greens, country lanes, and schoolyards. Stately year-round, the tree in its blazing autumn hue defines a New England fall. In the coastal South, massive evergreen live oaks form canopies to shade even the largest church picnic; draped with Spanish moss, they serve as icons of the region.

While large trees lend majesty and grandeur to a setting, smaller trees, such as flowering cherries, hawthorns, and dogwoods,

*Large trees, such as this red maple, lend grandeur to the landscape.*

*The romance of the coastal South is captured by this avenue of live oaks and their companion, Spanish moss.*

form an important link between a garden's "ceiling" and its "floor." Their size more closely mirrors human scale; their flowers, foliage, and fruit are within easy reach. These trees bring a sense of intimacy to the landscape, whether accenting an entry, providing a spot of shade, or creating a small space within a larger garden room.

This book will give you the information you need to select the best trees for your garden and will help you keep them in top condition. With this knowledge, your imagination will shape your plans; time and patience take care of the rest.

*The dogwood, best known for its white flowers in spring, should not be overlooked for its gifts of red berries and soft fall color.*

# Practical Benefits of Trees

*Trees are wonderful living tools. Employ them in your garden to provide both beauty and protection to the environment.*

*It takes 60 years for willow oaks to attain this size, but their magic is passed down to future generations.*

One of the benefits of trees is their ability to temper your immediate environment, no matter where you live. Tree plantings may result in measurable utility savings by shading your home during the summer while allowing the sun's warming rays to stream in during the winter. A row of dense evergreen trees on the northwest side of the yard can shield a Midwestern house from frigid winter winds. Dense plantings also shield beachfront homes and gardens from damaging salt spray. A well-placed screen of trees will prolong the life of the physical structure of your home by simply deflecting adverse weather conditions. You will find that you can employ trees not only for beauty but for practical purposes as well.

## Added Property Value

Perhaps the most subtle yet practical advantage to tree plantings is the long-term value trees lend to the property. Real estate professionals maintain that houses with trees are more desirable than comparable houses without them.

A well-tended canopy reinforces a community's sense of pride; tree-lined streets "speak" for the neighborhood. In suburbs of Atlanta and Birmingham, towering canopies of native loblolly pines shade entire neighborhoods with a roof of foliage at least 70 feet tall. These communities are among the most desirable and therefore most highly valued neighborhoods.

# Windbreaks

Evergreen trees, such as Norway spruce, white pine, or American holly, act as barriers to disrupt seasonal winds, protecting susceptible plants from windburn and winter wilting. Plant these evergreens as a windbreak on the northwest side of your garden, and they will protect both plants and people from high winds. These plantings can also be effective snowbreaks when planted in areas that are frequently blanketed with powder.

Trees also serve as useful beachfront windbreaks by reducing the erosion of loose sand by wind. They also help prevent winds from depositing sand where it is not wanted. Red cedar and Japanese black pine are two effective windbreaks; their low branches are close to the sand and prevent the wind from blowing the sand away. Where the prevailing winds stream parallel to the surf, plant a line of trees along the windward property line. This will keep upwind sand off your property and should slow the departure of your sand as well.

Beach windbreaks also thwart salt spray, a devastating corrosive to plants and soft metals, such as aluminum. Salt spray occurs along beaches where the wind blows in from the ocean. Plant salt-resistant trees, such as live oak, Southern magnolia, and red cedar, in dense groupings behind the front dunes to deflect salt-laden wind away from the house and garden. Select trees with multiple trunks and low branches for the most effective barriers. Plant a double row facing the ocean, with lower growing specimens in front of taller trees. In time, the salt spray will cause the trees to become a naturally sculpted fence.

# Natural Sound Barriers

You may also plant trees to help reduce traffic noise, but the planting should be so dense that you cannot easily walk through the trees and must be 50 to 75 feet wide to have any measurable effect. The trunks of pines threaded with vines work best to actually reduce noise; however, a dense row of trees provides psychological noise reduction—the out-of-sight, out-of-mind effect—that will encourage you to think the noise is diminished even if it is not.

*The dense foliage of Southern magnolia can help block the wind around a patio or deck. This tree also works well at the beach because of its tolerance to salt spray.*

# Take the Heat Off

When the temperature rises to 95 degrees, the heat in a vehicle can soar to more than 130 degrees. Not surprisingly, the first parking spaces claimed in a parking lot are those that are shaded. The shade of a tree can greatly reduce the air temperature inside a car, reducing the amount of heat that the seats, the steering wheel, and other surfaces absorb. When planted to cast shade over your driveway during the middle of the day, trees can provide great relief during the dog days of summer.

Check the sun's exact travel path by placing a tall marker, such as the handle of a broom, beside your driveway and marking its shadow at hourly intervals between 11:00 a.m. and 5:00 p.m., the hottest hours of the day. Use the shadow's path to locate the most effective place for a shade tree. Plant your tree so that it will stand between the driveway and the sun during these hours, typically on the south to southwest side of the parking area.

The drawback to planting trees near a driveway is that the tree's roots may spread beneath the pavement and crack the surface. Plant the tree at least 10 feet from the parking area to inhibit root growth under the pavement. Choose a tree that has an upright, ascending branching pattern, such as Chinese elm, sugar maple, or river birch. Avoid trees with lower branches that angle downward, such as pin oak and scarlet oak. Also, pines and red maples will drop sap, and fast-growing trees, such as silver maple, often have weak wood.

*Canopy trees are essential for creating a shade garden to cool you and your home.*

## Cooling Your Home

If your home has few trees around it, plant a combination of fast-growing trees, such as silver maple, and long-lived trees, such as willow oak or sugar maple. The fast-growing trees will provide quick shade until the more enduring species reach maturity.

Plant the trees at least 20 feet from the house so that their foliage will block the afternoon sun from shining on the roof. This reduces the build-up of heat in the attic. Try to position at least one tree so that it will shade your central air-conditioning unit, further decreasing your power bills.

## Growth in the Shade

The trees in your yard reduce the amount of direct sunlight that reaches the ground, allowing the ground to retain moisture that would otherwise evaporate. The shade cast by these trees promotes the growth of small, shade-loving trees, such as dogwoods. Large trees often provide such dense shade that lawn grasses will not grow; however, some trees cast a light shade that allows lawn growth while still reducing evaporation. River birch and most pines permit enough sunlight to filter through so that grass will grow.

A small tree, such as crape myrtle, redbud, or Yoshino cherry, can reduce the bleaching effect of direct sunlight on interior furnishings and floor finishes. Plant these trees near windows so that their foliage blocks or diffuses direct rays. See pages 18–20 for more information on shade trees.

See pages 18–20 for more information on shade trees.

## COOL IN THE CITY

Trees benefit metropolitan areas in much the same way they do neighborhoods.

• They are attractive.

• They absorb pollutants by processing carbon dioxide and releasing water vapor.

• Their shade cools parking areas and office buildings by as much as 10 degrees.

## GOOD TREES, QUICK SHADE

| Tree | Height after 10 Years | Spread after 10 Years | Density of Shade | Form |
|---|---|---|---|---|
| Bald cypress | 25 to 35 feet | 10 to 15 feet | Light to moderate | Conical, pyramidal |
| Chinese elm | 30 to 40 feet | 20 to 25 feet | Light to moderate | Rounded, spreading |
| Crape myrtle | 15 to 25 feet | 10 to 15 feet | Light | Upright, spreading |
| Pin oak | 30 to 35 feet | 15 to 20 feet | Moderate to heavy | Pyramidal |
| Red maple | 30 to 35 feet | 15 to 20 feet | Moderate to heavy | Pyramidal, oval |
| Red oak | 30 to 35 feet | 20 to 25 feet | Moderate to heavy | Rounded |
| River birch | 30 to 35 feet | 15 to 20 feet | Moderate | Upright |
| Tulip poplar | 35 to 40 feet | 15 to 20 feet | Light to moderate | Upright |
| Willow oak | 30 to 35 feet | 20 to 25 feet | Moderate | Rounded |

## Trees Define Spaces

You may also use trees to define space. On an average residential lot, any group of three or more trees begins to define space by being a self-contained group within the garden. Individual trees bring different character to the spaces they define. If you plant a grove of flowering dogwoods or saucer magnolias informally in the open lawn, they imply a space without rigidly defining it. These ornamental trees will create a restful mood and a feeling of welcome.

Three large trees grouped together can have a different impact. The large trunks will form a protective enclosure, while the towering canopies reinforce a feeling of invincibility. This arrangement forms a natural space for a treehouse or a child's fortress. Tree plantings that are matched on either side of a walkway become an alley, a narrow passageway defined and enclosed by the trunks and foliage. These trees reinforce the geometry of the garden.

*As it grows, this young tree will reinforce a sense of space created by a bed of ground cover. Ground covers are an effective way to tie together separate trees.*

## Evergreens for Screening

Trees may also be planted to form a natural barrier between your yard and the rest of the world. Unlike a fence, which is often subject to design or height restrictions, trees may grow to heights far beyond those allowed for fencing. Evergreens used as screen plantings at the edge of a garden also become a backdrop against which other garden elements may be positioned. The flowers of a Yoshino cherry will stand out against the dark backdrop of a red cedar screen. In winter, the light gray bark of the cherry will be sharply defined. Evergreen trees sustain garden form during the winter months and are useful as visual anchors in the cold season. They may also serve as windbreaks.

Few trees are as effective, fast, and reliable for screening as native pines. Loblolly pine is dense and full when young and will be a good 15-foot screen for 10 to 15 years before growing to its mature height. White pine provides an effective barrier from the ground to 40 to 60 feet. Leyland cypress, the champion for quick cover in narrow, sunny spaces, also makes a nice screen. If you can wait for slow-growing trees, consider the long-lived evergreen hollies, such as American holly, Foster holly, and Savannah holly, with their glossy foliage and bright berries. These trees also add winter interest for gardeners and for wildlife.

*Evergreen hollies serve as an effective screen and reinforce a garden entry.*

## Trees with Prominence

The trees that line roads and driveways create a formal sense of entrance. You can capture this feeling on a suburban lot by lining the drive with crape myrtles; along country drives, plant sugar maples to establish the transition of entry. A double row of Savannah hollies or tulip poplars creates a space that you want to walk through.

Use evergreen trees to frame your view of the garden from indoors. Plant three evergreens in an extended triangle, with the closest and farthest trees on the same side of the garden and an intermediate tree on the opposite side. Your eye will naturally scan from tree to tree, reviewing the open garden room that they frame.

A large, solitary evergreen, such as white pine, Norway spruce, or live oak, can become the dominant element in the winter landscape. Give this centerpiece a prominent position and room to grow; plant it at least 30 feet from other trees.

*The "roof" provided by these shade trees makes this house appear small, friendly, and intimate.*

# Sense of Scale

Trees are important tools for creating a sense of scale in the landscape. Scale refers to the sense of proportion between objects, an important relationship in gardens since this perception determines the "feel" of a garden. Items that are too large for their perceived space may be intimidating; small elements in large areas may disappear. While trees will not change the actual size of the objects, they can provide visual balance between the object, the viewer, and the setting.

## Using Large Trees for Scale

A large house on the crown of a treeless hill may be rather imposing. The same house viewed through the foliage of large trees is softened and made less intimidating. The trees provide a foreground for the view of the house. Groupings of trees make large spaces seem friendlier by filling them, thereby making them less vast. Such plantings also provide a reference for both distance and depth perception.

## Using Small Trees for Scale

You can reverse this trick to make a small house appear larger. Use small trees with a canopy of foliage that reaches just below the eaves of the house. This makes the house seem larger, as it is taller than the trees.

In addition to their decorative value, small ornamental trees can help you make small garden spaces seem larger. Anything viewed at a distance appears to be small. If you plant a small tree at the rear of a small property, it will appear to be farther away than it is, thereby increasing the perception of depth in the garden. This illusion is enhanced when large trees are planted near the viewer.

## Scale Within a Neighborhood

Tree plantings reinforce the sense of individuality in new neighborhoods where the houses look similar. If you live in a community where the homes are large but are built on small lots, plant a mix of evergreen and deciduous trees to set your house apart from the others. Use fast-growing evergreens, such as pines, to give your house a backdrop. Use willow oak or red maple to shade and frame your house and then add smaller ornamental trees for pizzazz.

As far as proportion and scale are concerned, what is good for the home is even better for the entire neighborhood. Nothing is more effective for providing a sense of scale than a uniform planting of trees. In a new neighborhood with few trees, a uniform street-tree planting will quickly bring a sense of community to the neighborhood, linking the homes to one another.

## Guidelines for Planting Street Trees

If you approach your neighbors to begin a street-tree planting, be sure to check with city officials about any restrictions that may frustrate your efforts. Keep the following points in mind:

• Choose trees that are well adapted to your environment so that they will fend off cold, heat, drought, and pests without special care.

• When planting large trees, be sure to select long-lived ones, such as oaks or maples.

• Do not plan to use Bradford pear, silver maple, or pines for long-term plantings as they are weak wooded and frequently split in storms.

• Look for trees that have ascending branches; these form tall, spreading canopies under which you can park and walk. Rounded trees, such as willow oak, make better street trees than pin oak and weeping willow, which have long branches that sweep the ground.

• Do not plant red maple, sugar maple, dogwood, or sourwood along streets in city centers. These trees suffer scorched leaves and dead branches in hot, urban conditions.

### RECOMMENDED LARGE STREET TREES

Bald cypress
Littleleaf linden
Live oak
Male ginkgo
Red maple
Red oak
Shumard oak
Sugar maple
Willow oak

### RECOMMENDED SMALL STREET TREES

Crabapple
Crape myrtle
Kwanzan cherry
Redbud
Sourwood

### UNDESIRABLE STREET TREES

Bradford pear—weak wood
Female ginkgo—messy fruit
Pin oak—branches hang to the
    ground
Pine—weak wood, pinecones
Silver maple—weak wood,
    surface roots

*Good street-tree plantings can minimize an uncommonly wide public right of way and give the neighborhood an intimate feel.*

# Aesthetic Benefits of Trees

*Paint a garden portrait with the flowers, the foliage, and the fruit of trees. They add color and texture that change with the seasons while providing a year-round framework for the landscape.*

Every tree species lends individual charm to the garden, whether it offers reliable shade, a distinctive branching habit, showy flowers, or magnificent fall color. In addition to their practical benefits, trees add character and style to your garden. The variety among species—form, foliage, flowers, even bark—makes choosing one tree very difficult. However, the right tree determines a garden's look and feel. In this respect, trees are the clothing of the garden; you can dress things up with American holly or Bradford pear, be a bit boisterous with the explosive blooms of crape myrtle, or tone down the formality by planting Leyland cypress or crabapple. Some trees, such as dogwood, are both casual and elegant within the garden scheme.

*Flowering trees, such as crape myrtles, may be the most outstanding of all landscape plants because the blooms are an added bonus.*

# The Color Palette

Sometimes, in your effort to create drama in the landscape, you may underestimate the simple contributions a tree can make. One fact that many gardeners overlook is that the foliage of every tree has distinctive hues that vary throughout the tree's life cycle. In early spring, the new leaves of a sugar maple emerge as washed, soft pastels; by fall, the same tree blazes in orange and red. Some trees retain a purple leaf color throughout the growing season.

Sycamore has light green foliage that contrasts with the deeper lustrous green of white oak, the leaves of which emerge as a soft russet red. The steadiest greens during the growing season are the leaves of sweet gum, sugar maple, and white ash. Loblolly pine has a yellowish-green hue, while white pine is more bluish green. Native Virginia pine is dark green with a hint of yellow.

Plant lighter green trees in the back of the garden to make the space seem smaller. Use dark green-gray foliage, which seems to recede, to make the garden appear larger. Plant contrasting greens to create a play of colors that will break up the uniformity of your garden. Purple or red leaves will always be accents in the landscape.

*The greatest contribution of trees to the landscape is their many shades of foliage.*

# Forms of Trees

The most enduring aspect of a tree is its form. Although deciduous trees shed their leaves in winter, their shapes are still distinctive even when their branches are bare. The typical form of a tree is as immutable as a fingerprint; gardeners rely on the fact that all Bradford pears, for instance, will grow to look alike. Seven standard tree forms are described here; an eighth category includes those trees that have no distinct form.

*The true form of a tree is revealed in winter, outlined and emphasized by snow.*

• **Oval.** These good shade trees are quite effective when planted in the open lawn. American beech, willow oak, sugar maple, and white oak have this form.

• **Upright, rounded.** Slightly taller than they are broad, these trees look natural in groves. Bradford pear, tulip poplar, red maple, and loblolly pine are examples. These are excellent trees for lining a country drive-way or for planting as a natural-istic group.

• **Vase shaped.** The classic shape of the American elm, this form is prized for its grace and dignity as a street tree. Chinese elm, Kwanzan cherry, and red-bud all have this form. Plant these trees beside a sidewalk, a driveway, or a patio; you can easily walk beneath them.

• **Linear, upright.** These trees provide strong vertical lines in the landscape. Single-trunked river birch and Leyland cypress have this form; they work well silhou-etted against architecture.

• **Conical.** This is a powerful form for use as an accent in the landscape. Plant conical trees at the corner of the house or as punctuation in a garden bed. American holly and Foster holly are conical forms.

• **Pendulous.** Also visually riveting, these trees suggest grace and motion. Plant a tree with pendulous form as a single specimen in a corner of the garden or at the end of a driveway or a sidewalk. Weeping cherry is a common example.

• **Spreading.** This is an elegant form with branches that are as broad as the tree is tall. Live oak, dogwood, and Yoshino cherry are trees with spreading forms. Plant large trees singly; smaller specimens work well as accents to other trees.

• **Erratic or irregular forms.** Some species of trees do not grow into a specific form. Ginkgo and white pine are examples. Use these trees at the end of a line of sight, such as the end of a driveway.

*The form of a spreading tree, such as this cherry, is most pronounced while in full bloom and foliage.*

## All Shade Is Not Alike

Just as the foliage and the form of trees differ, so does the quality of the shade beneath their branches. The amount of shade that a tree brings to the garden will have an impact on many aspects of life within the garden.

## Leaf Size

A tree's shade depends upon the size and density of its leaves: the finer the foliage, the lighter the shade and the better the planting underneath. River birch and loblolly pine produce this light shade, which is desirable for outdoor sitting areas. Large-leafed trees, such as sugar maple, sycamore, and Southern magnolia, cast a deep, dark shade that makes planting beneath the tree more challenging. Plant these trees at the edge of the garden if you do not want to remove their lower limbs.

## Open or Closed Shade

The higher the branches, the more open the shade. Mature loblolly pines and willow oaks have high limbs (above 30 feet), permitting diffuse, bright light but little direct, hot sun to reach the ground. This is ideal shade for growing shade-loving plants. River birch also produces effective, open shade for decks and patios.

*The high limbs of loblolly pines cast ideal light shade for a dogwood.*

Southern magnolia and American holly bear low branches, casting a deep, closed shade. Even if you remove their lower limbs, the shade is still very dark and difficult for other plants to live beneath. Plant these trees as open-lawn specimens or anchors in the garden border. Avoid trying to plant anything in their shade. Older live oaks, however, offer ideal shade for shrubs or perennials but can be too dark for lawn grasses.

Do not plant shade-loving plants beneath young shade trees right away; new trees do not produce protective shade immediately.

## Deciduous or Evergreen

Shade beneath a deciduous tree is deepest during the summer, when the sun is high overhead. Place shrubs that need protection from direct sun in beds under deciduous trees. Some direct sun will slant beneath the canopy early and late in the day; this helps flowering shrubs develop more buds.

During the winter months, the sun is lower in the sky and casts longer shadows. Deciduous trees have shed their leaves, so their bare branches cast a more delicate shade. This shadow pattern is a decorative accent for your winter garden.

Evergreen trees maintain a more constant shade year-round. American holly, Southern magnolia, and live oak cast a very deep shade; needle-leafed evergreens cast the most desirable shade, one that filters severe sun while permitting sufficient light for shrubs and flowers that need partial shade.

## Upright or Spreading

The form and size of a tree determine the size and shape of its shade pattern. Narrow upright trees, such as Leyland cypress and red cedar, offer little shade when planted singly; when several are planted as a privacy screen, their combined shade has increased cooling power. Trees with spreading crowns, such as willow oak or sugar maple, will shade an entire yard. Plant three or more in a zigzag pattern with at least 35 feet between them. If you plant shade trees closer than 35 feet apart, be prepared to thin them.

*In winter, deciduous trees create filigree against the sky.*

## Getting the Most from Shade Trees

The harshest summer sun shines from the south-southwest between noon and 5:00 p.m. To create a shade planting, you must position trees so that they shade the bed during these hours. A high canopy tree, such as river birch or Chinese elm, will work well.

*No tree can hold a candle to Japanese maple in fall.*

Plant trees to shade your patio or deck during the hours you are most likely to be there, generally the early evening. Use a tree that casts a deeper shade, such as red maple or sugar maple, as its canopy will block the low-angled late-afternoon sun.

# Fall Color

About 30 species of deciduous trees are responsible for the vivid array of fall color. They depend upon a combination of sunny summer weather, moderate rainfall during the growing season, and cool, dry fall days with bright sun for the best color.

There is no one way to use trees with vibrant fall color, although you might want to bear in mind the color of your home. Trees that turn yellow look better against red brick than those that smolder dark red to crimson.

Plant smaller trees, such as redbud, dogwood, or Bradford pear, in front of an evergreen backdrop to make the color seem more vivid. Similarly, mix small trees with pines. To brighten a garden corner, plant a tree with yellow fall color, such as sugar maple, ginkgo,

*This tapestry of sugar maples shows all of the tree's fall hues.*

or redbud. If the fall color of your shade trees is predominantly yellow, plant contrasting small trees in front of them, such as dogwood or Yoshino cherry.

Single specimens in a lawn can be unmatched for streetside appeal. Use a ginkgo or a bronze beech for dramatic golden highlights. A country lane lined with sugar maples can be the inspiration for planting these trees streetside in your neighborhood. Small trees that seem to have fall color pooling along the leaf veins, such as Japanese maple, are better appreciated up close, such as beside a patio, a sidewalk, or an entry.

Remember, the more fall color, the better. A tree border can be a scramble of fall color to match the exuberance of the season. The most spectacular fall tree is sugar maple (yellow to orange), native throughout the East. Sugar maple is followed closely by the compound-leafed hickories (amber to gold) which have the greatest range of yellows. In the deep South, red maple (yellow to scarlet), ginkgo (golden yellow), and American beech, which turns a golden bronze, are very reliable.

Equally dependable are four small trees: sassafras (yellow to bright orange), flowering dogwood (crimson), redbud (lemon yellow), and sourwood (maroon, with ivory, pearl-like strands of seed capsules).

Oaks sport a range of fall colors from deep red (red oak) to rust red (white oak) to vivid scarlet (scarlet oak). Generally, oaks reach better color in northern latitudes. Black gums, with shiny red leaves, stand out when planted among oaks because of the metallic quality of their leaves.

*Japanese maple may be used effectively as an accent planting. The foliage is handsome during the growing season but is especially expressive in fall.*

## WHY LEAVES CHANGE COLOR

If you have ever noticed the many soft pastel greens of new leaves in spring, you have observed a valuable clue about the mechanism of fall color. The characteristic color of a tree species in autumn is due to pigments that are present in the leaf throughout the year. The first hint of fall color occurs in the new foliage of early spring: you will see that white oak has a russet flush and red maple has a reddish cast. Some trees have chemical compounds that make reds; some have compounds that produce yellow and orange, and others make brown.

During the growing season, the substance that enables plants to convert carbon dioxide and water into food, *chlorophyll,* is continually replenished. This green substance masks most other pigments from view. As fall approaches and the leaves reach the end of their life cycle, chlorophyll is no longer replenished. When the chlorophyll disappears, the previously masked pigments become visible.

## Flowers

Flowers are the most popular ornamental contribution a tree makes to the garden. While fall color occurs all at once, flowers bloom at different times during the growing season. To vary the display of blooms in your garden, plant trees that flower at different times during the season, from the very early flowers of red maple to the late summer flowers of sourwood and crape myrtle. Early-blooming saucer magnolia may be followed by Bradford pear, redbud, Yoshino cherry, flowering dogwood, and Kousa dogwood for a continuous array of blooms.

## Add Variety

Choosing different species of flowering trees adds variety in both color and form and brings different moods to the garden. Saucer magnolias have huge, tulip-shaped flowers that look like candelabra while Yoshino cherry has delicate pink-white flowers.

Flowering dogwood and crape myrtle are excellent specimen trees that convey vastly different moods. Dogwood blossoms float like great snowflakes and impart serenity to the garden while crape myrtle is festive, bursting against the hot sky like a midsummer firecracker. Crabapple and Kwanzan cherry are showy specimens, but Yoshino cherry, alone or in a group, seems delicate, refined, and reflective. Keep this tone in mind when selecting trees for your garden.

*A young crape myrtle lifts its flowers in a small entry garden.*

## Change Points of Interest

Do not put all of your flowering trees in one place; position them throughout the garden to highlight different areas. Early-flowering trees, such as red maple or star magnolia, placed in a favorite view can help chase away winter's blues. Use summer-flowering plants next to an outdoor sitting area so that you can enjoy them throughout the warm season.

## Color Your World

Trees that have a single flower on each twig, such as dogwood, saucer lily, and Loebner magnolia, appear more graceful when seen against a dark backdrop. Plant these trees in front of an evergreen screen or a dark wall.

Trees with *aggregate* flowers, those that are clustered together, do not need a contrasting backdrop to have vivid impact. Examples of these are the crabapples and the cherries, which are lovely in most settings.

Trees that flower after their leaves emerge, such as Kousa dogwood, hawthorn, and crape myrtle, work well as specimen plants. Trees with very vivid colors need a complementary background— avoid planting deep red crape myrtles in front of a red brick wall, for example.

## Seasonal Peaks

Just because a tree's blooms are attractive does not mean it is outstanding in other seasons, an observation that should guide its use in the landscape. Crabapples and oriental magnolias decline in landscape interest after flowering. Plant them in a border or at the garden's edge so that their flowers may be enjoyed but their location in the garden is not central. Dogwood, hawthorn, and crape myrtle have many desirable features in addition to their flowers and are quite suitable for garden center stage.

# Fruit

Fruit follows flowers in the horticultural world, and the fruit of some trees is as spectacular as the blooms. Many trees bear rather unusual fruit, which is a welcome feature during the dormant months.

*Hawthorns produce a soft show of flowers in spring followed by exquisite berries in the fall.*

*The curling, multicolored bark of a young river birch is its most lovely feature.*

Brightly colored berries adorn the hollies and decorate the winter landscape. Possum haw and winterberry are two deciduous hollies with spectacular berries, so showy that they have gained favor as substitutes for crabapples. Of course, the familiar American holly and its many selections have long been seasonal favorites.

Both dogwood and Washington hawthorn have bright red berries, making them popular ornamentals through winter. Birds also enjoy their berries. If these trees are visible from the house, you may watch cedar waxwings, grosbeaks, and robins swoop to a brightly colored meal.

*Crabapple makes its best show in late summer and fall when the fruit turns bright red.*

Some fruits are unexpectedly beautiful. Pods of the deciduous magnolias look like upright candlesticks in summer. The samaras of a maple are a child's favorite when they whirl to the ground in early spring like small propeller-driven flying machines. The fruit of sourwood resembles strings of pearls, and the red crabapples hang like ornaments from the branches.

## Beware of Falling Fruit

Oaks, sweet gum, and the female ginkgo have fruit with an aggravating downside. Every acorn that is not swept away in fall becomes an unwanted sprout in spring. Sweet-gum balls are the bane of any barefoot pedestrian, but the worst fruit problem is that of the female gingko, which has a sulfurous odor. Do not plant a fruit-dropping tree near an area where you walk.

## Bark

Do not overlook the bark of a tree for its beauty and ability to attract attention. This is a subtle contribution that brings ornamentation to small courtyard gardens and adds character to the winter landscape. Plant trees with unusual bark in locations that allow close viewing.

*Chinese elm is instantly recognized by the pattern of its bark.*

Use bark texture, color, and pattern to guide your choice of specimen plantings, such as the feature tree in a courtyard, next to a patio, or near an entry.

Bark with a bold pattern or rugged texture has a strong ornamental effect. You may enjoy the curling, flaky bark of river birch or the mottled red-and-cream coloration of crape myrtle from across the garden. The same is true of Chinese elm, with its patchy bark, and sourwood, which has deeply furrowed bark. Red maple and American beech have ornamental bark along their upper branches, which is visible from as much as a block away. This is also true of the white upper bark of sycamore.

Japanese maple and flowering dogwood feature more subtle bark, though it is also quite striking. Flowering dogwood has a patterned trunk with gray upper branches. Japanese maple is most appreciated in a courtyard or along a sidewalk, within 10 to 15 feet of the viewer. This tree has smooth, evenly colored bark with new twigs flushed either green or red, depending on the selection.

## Evergreens in Winter

Evergreen trees become particularly important to the landscape during the winter months. Even when used primarily as a backdrop planting or to screen unpleasant views, their foliage and form set them apart when other trees and shrubs are without leaves.

Evergreens keep their color and form throughout the winter months. Some hollies will turn even deeper in color, causing the berries to appear brighter, and other hollies turn from green to purple with the cold. High overhead, pine trees, one of the most valuable evergreen groups, display cones.

Review your landscape in winter to see if you need evergreen trees, either for privacy or for ornamental purposes. If so, plant a fast-growing evergreen, such as Leyland cypress, to quickly fill in the landscape. Consider additional evergreens for their aesthetic contributions, either as a backdrop for the bark or fruit of specimen trees or to frame a particular garden vista, such as a gazebo or a fountain. Finally, look at your garden to see if you need a specimen evergreen, such as American holly, to serve as the focal point of winter interest. Winter is the time to bring the brightness of holly berries into the otherwise gray garden.

*The full form of an evergreen holly naturally takes prominence in winter.*

# Trees in the Landscape

*Trees frame the view of a home and anchor the surrounding beds. (From left:* flowering dogwood, Rotunda holly, flowering cherry, dwarf winged euonymus, juniper*)*

*Before you plant, be sure the trees you choose will suit your garden's needs and provide the look you want.*

Unfortunately, you must temper your ideal garden selections with horticultural reality and practicality. There is no sense in planting today what will be troublesome tomorrow. Bear in mind the climate and conditions of your garden, including the following key considerations, as you select the best trees to plant.

# Height

A medium or large tree will grow 40 to 70 feet tall. A two-story house is usually about 30 feet in height. If you want to shade the roof, you need a lot of foliage above the roofline, not just the top twigs. To shade a house, choose a tall tree, such as sycamore or red maple, that will naturally grow taller than your home.

Here are some of the finest small trees that will grow under public utility lines. Such lines may be service lines to the rear of the property or the streetside phone and power lines. Before planting, always check with your local power company about specific restrictions.

Carolina silverbell
Chinese fringe tree*
Chinese pistache
Crape myrtle*
Franklin tree
Fringe tree*
Ironwood
Japanese maple*
Japanese snowbell
Kousa dogwood*
Loquat
Oriental magnolias*
Paperbark maple
Purple-leafed plum
Redbud*
Smoke tree
Sourwood*
Yaupon holly

* Profiled in this book.

Small trees, such as crape myrtle and redbud, rarely exceed 25 feet in height. While they have terrific landscape value, their shade and scale provision limits them to an outdoor sitting area or an entry. These trees are particularly useful for areas under power lines. When selecting a small tree to plant near a walkway, choose one with branches that ascend from at least 4 feet above the base. These high branches will be easier to walk under as the tree matures.

## Spread

Except for trees with narrow, conical forms, such as Leyland cypress, most large trees will grow a crown much wider than 25 to 30 feet. Since average residential lots are about 60 feet wide and the house is generally no more than 50 feet from the street, two large trees, such as willow oaks or sugar maples, will grow to shade the entire front yard.

The recommended separation between willow oaks is 40 feet, although 60 feet is preferred. Stick to the recommended spacing despite the fact that the 10-foot-tall tree you plant may seem small. Remind yourself that trees, like children, grow up very quickly. Redbud, a fast-growing small tree, will be 20 feet wide in 10 to 15 years. Except for special landscape effects, such as privacy plantings, you should space all trees at least 20 feet from one another for the long-term health of the trees.

## Roots

The roots of a large tree grow far beyond the reach of the longest branch. A tree's roots can crack driveways and sidewalks, and may even weaken the foundation of your home. Allow at least 10 feet between a large tree and the driveway. Do not plant a large tree between the sidewalk and the curb, as it will certainly crack the sidewalk. Plant shade trees no closer than 15 to 20 feet from the foundation of a house.

Never use willow oak, red maple, river birch, or silver maple near a septic drain field. Around older houses, these fast-growing species may clog terra-cotta drain lines. Fortunately, the use of PVC pipe for drainage around newer homes has virtually eliminated this threat.

Give a tree enough room to get a grip in the earth. The root system must be strong enough to resist the pressure of high, gusty winds. Large trees that are planted closer than 15 feet to the house will be deprived of critical space for root growth that will anchor the tree.

## Soil Conditions

If you are able to match a tree's natural soil conditions, you will successfully grow it in your garden. Trees that can tolerate low oxygen are the best choices for heavy clay or compacted urban soil where there is very little air space in the soil. River birch and sycamore are good choices for moist or intermittently wet soils.

When a lot is cleared for the building of a house, most of the fertile topsoil is removed. The subsoil that is exposed is severely compacted. Hardy tree species, such as loblolly pine, sassafras, red maple, and redbud, are among the best trees to plant in the disrupted soil surrounding a new home.

Few soil conditions are as nightmarish as a highly eroded topsoil layer above heavy clay subsoil. Without sufficient topsoil or easily penetrable subsoil, a tree's roots may emerge at the surface. You will need to add topsoil to the area before planting.

Soil that is highly alkaline calls for trees that do not need acid soil to grow. Red maple and red cedar, which are native in regions with alkaline soils, adapt well.

## Rate of Growth

Many trees that grow rapidly do so at the expense of wood strength. Silver maple, hybrid poplar, and Bradford pear grow several feet per year, but they have weak wood and an invasive root system. Among the most dependable fast-growing trees are red maple, river birch, tulip poplar, white pine, loblolly pine, pin oak, red oak, willow oak, and Chinese elm. Bear in mind that a tree grows more rapidly during the first 15 years. Also, the larger the tree when planted, the more difficulty it will have adjusting to transplanting.

## Longevity

The massive, awe-inspiring trees, such as sugar maple, American beech, live oak, white oak, red cedar, and Southern magnolia, take decades to grow to spectacular form. These trees will live for a century or more. Accordingly, plant them in protected spots that are likely to be undisturbed so that future generations may admire your gift in years to come.

Short-lived, fast-growing trees can be useful as well. They offer quick solutions to immediate problems, such as serving as a privacy screen. Plant an otherwise undesirable tree, such as silver maple, if you need results now. If there is room, mix short-lived and long-lived species together and thin the planting as the trees grow.

## LONG-LIVED SPECIES

The following trees will outlive your great-great-grandchildren:

| Tree | Mature Height |
|------|---------------|
| Bald cypress | 50 to 80 feet |
| Beech | 60 to 80 feet |
| Canadian hemlock | 40 to 70 feet |
| Chinese elm | 40 to 50 feet |
| Crape myrtle | 15 to 30 feet |
| Ginkgo (male) | 50 to 80 feet |
| Hickory | 60 to 80 feet |
| Live oak | 40 to 80 feet |
| Norway spruce | 40 to 80 feet |
| Pin oak | 60 to 80 feet |
| Red cedar | 40 to 50 feet |
| Red maple | 40 to 60 feet |
| Red oak | 60 to 80 feet |
| Shumard oak | 50 to 80 feet |
| Sugar maple | 50 to 80 feet |
| White oak | 60 to 100 feet |
| Willow oak | 60 to 80 feet |

*River birch will become a large shade tree in 5 to 10 years.*

# Getting Started

*Deciding which species is right for you is just the beginning; picking out a healthy specimen is the key to realizing your ideal landscape.*

*Always peel the burlap away from the trunk and fold it down so that none is left protruding above the soil line. Burlap exposed to air will keep moisture away from the root ball.*

When selecting a tree, remember that bigger is not necessarily better. In fact, a small tree, one less than 2 inches in trunk diameter and between 8 to 10 feet in height, is less expensive, transplants more easily and safely, and will often outgrow a 12- to 16-foot tree that is planted at the same time.

## Handling a Tree

To avoid causing injury to the tree after purchase, always lift it by the root ball or the container; never pull the trunk. If you lift the tree by its trunk, the weight of the soil may tear the feeder roots.

Load the trees on your truck by placing the canopy next to the cab to shield the foliage from the wind. If you cannot position the tree this way, protect its leaves or needles by wrapping the tree in burlap or an old sheet. You do not need to wrap the tree if you are travelling a short distance at residential speed.

Once you get home, promptly plant the tree. If you are unable to plant it immediately, set the tree upright in a shady place and keep the roots moist and mulched.

## Preparing the Soil

If you have very poor soil or subsoil exposed by erosion or grading, prepare a wide planting area by tilling in topsoil at least 8 inches deep in an area three to five times the width of the root ball.

If you are planting a single tree, dig a hole at least twice as wide as the root ball but no deeper. Take the edge of the shovel and slice into the sides of the hole; the looser the surrounding soil, the faster the roots will penetrate.

Amend the soil with organic matter, particularly near the beach. Sand has no organic matter to promote plant growth. Heavy clay subsoils also need organic supplements. Pulverized pine bark, often labeled "soil conditioner," helps loosen clay to provide space for air and water.

## Planting a Tree

Trees for sale may be packaged in one of three ways: bare root, balled and burlapped, or container grown. Below are some guidelines for handling and planting each.

### Bare-Root Trees

Bare-root trees are exactly that—the roots are bare of soil. These are generally sold in late winter and should be planted immediately lest the roots, which are usually packaged in moss or sawdust and wrapped tightly in plastic, dry out. Bare-root trees are generally lower priced, spring-flowering trees or seedlings grown and sold by the forestry service.

For bare-root trees, pile soil in the hole to create a mound over which you may spread the roots. While holding the plant upright, backfill the hole, making sure that the root crown sits slightly higher than the surrounding soil. Tamp the soil in place with your foot, then water thoroughly, removing all air pockets. Plant bare-root trees as soon as possible or tuck them into compost or pulverized bark if you cannot plant immediately.

## Balled-and-Burlapped Trees

A balled-and-burlapped tree is dug from a field; its root ball is held together with a burlap wrap. Leave the burlap on the plant, as it helps keep the root ball intact. Set the plant in the hole so that the top of the root ball is level with the soil. When the plant is at the proper height, peel the burlap down around the sides of the root ball.

Never leave the burlap exposed above the surface as it will draw moisture away from the root ball. While cotton burlap decomposes, roots will not easily penetrate synthetic or treated burlap. Make three or four vertical slices through the material before refilling the hole so that the roots will pierce the wrapping.

Refill the hole with soil, mounding it over the sides of the exposed root ball, and water thoroughly.

## Container-Grown Trees

Plant a container-grown tree much the same way as you would one that is balled and burlapped. Dig a hole no deeper than the container and then remove the container, being careful not to damage the roots. For seedling-sized trees, turn the container upside down, cover the top of the root ball with your hand, and gently slide the container off the roots. Lay larger, heavier plants on their sides and slip off the container. If the roots are growing through the drainage holes in the container, you will have to cut the container off the plant with a pocketknife.

If the roots are matted and tangled, spread them out by cutting crosswise through the bottom third of the root ball, making sure no large roots grow in a circle around the plant. After removing the tree, set it in the hole so that the top of the root ball is level with the soil; then backfill and water.

## SELECTING A TREE

Most large shade trees are grown in fields before they are sold in nurseries. As their canopies grow, so do their root systems. When a tree is dug for sale, part of its expansive root system is left in the field. The tree will spend the next several years trying to replace its roots instead of growing new branches.

Small trees, especially those grown in containers, have smaller root systems than large trees. When dug for transplanting, the root system will stay intact. These trees will grow at a faster rate than larger trees because they will not need to replace missing roots.

For this reason, the most satisfactory selection is a tree grown in a container. If you cannot find a container-grown tree, look for a tree with a solid ball of earth around it. If the root ball is cracked, crumbling, or sandy, or has visible cut roots, choose another plant. Avoid purchasing trees with trunks that wobble or seem unsteady.

# Caring for Trees

*Proper planting is the first step to successful growth.*

Fall is the best time of year to plant a tree because the soil is warm enough to allow root growth but the top is not producing new foliage. Do not plant trees in late spring or summer. When newly planted, a tree will not have a fully established root system. The roots provide the tree the water it needs; without a well-established root system, the tree will not survive the heat of summer. However the tree you bring home is packaged, there are certain steps you must take to ensure that it will thrive.

## Mulching

It is a good idea to apply a 3-inch layer of mulch around the base of a newly planted tree rather than allowing your lawn to come right up to the trunk. The mulch should extend at least a foot or two from the base of the plant. This will reduce the chance of *allelopathy,* a condition that occurs when some plants (in this case, grass) release chemicals that inhibit the growth of another plant (the newly planted tree). Mulching also helps keep the soil around the new roots cooler in summer and warmer in winter and reduces moisture loss during periods of drought.

## Supporting

Most trees that can be easily transported and planted rarely need staking. However, if the tree is very tall or in an area with strong prevailing winds, such as the oceanfront, you will want to stake it.

Staking kits, available at most landscape nurseries, will help protect fragile trees. The best staking system employs three stakes arranged equilaterally around the tree. Never use wire directly on the tree. Instead, loop a length of garden hose to the trunk, preferably at the first branch. By implanting the stakes within the mulched area at the base of the tree, you will eliminate the frustration of trying to mow around them.

## Protect the Trunks of Young Trees

Use purchased tree wraps to prevent the bark of young trees from splitting in freezing weather. If the newly planted tree is exposed to morning sun in winter, wrap the trunk lightly, removing the wrapping when the leaves emerge. Never leave the wrap on for longer than one year; this may encourage borers.

*Properly caring for your tree ensures its viability for years to come.*

# Watering

There is no substitute for watering newly planted trees directly with a hose. This ensures that water does indeed penetrate into the planting hole where the new roots are growing. A lawn sprinkler or a sprinkler system may not deliver adequate water to a newly planted tree where the water is most needed. Water gently, not at full pressure, for a few minutes no more than twice weekly.

# Fertilizing

The purpose of fertilizing is to meet a tree's nutritional needs. The easiest and most sensible approach to fertilization is to add nutrients to the soil before you plant. In most cases, a premium-quality, balanced fertilizer will suffice. Add compost or other organic matter, and then work a slow-release fertilizer into the soil before planting to ensure a constant supply of essential elements. Choose a fertilizer that contains at least half of its nitrogen in a slow-release form.

## The Fertilizer Label

By law, all fertilizers must carry a label stating the percentage of nutrients they contain. The three numbers always represent the percentage of nitrogen (N), phosphorus (P), and potassium (K). If the package is labeled 10-5-8, it contains 10 percent nitrogen, 5 percent phosphorus, and 8 percent potassium. These are the nutrients most important to a plant, so the combination of nitrogen, phosphorus, and potassium makes up what is called a *complete fertilizer.*

*The first watering will help the soil to settle around the root ball.*

Nitrogen stimulates new growth, especially early foliage, which is why you need a good supply early in the growth cycle. Because nitrogen is very soluble and mobile in the soil, you should buy a product that contains a slow-release form. Otherwise, your nitrogen may be washed away before being absorbed.

Phosphorus is essential for overall plant health and encourages flowering. However, too much phosphorus in the soil blocks the plant's ability to absorb other nutrients. Unless your soil test indicates a deficiency, use a fertilizer low in phosphorus. Many suburban soils may be high in phosphorus if the land was once agricultural.

Potassium, also called potash on fertilizer labels, is essential to plant metabolism. It is crucial to a plant's cell wall structure as well as its ability to manufacture food. Do not use potassium in excess as it may burn your plants.

*You may prune small, low limbs with a pole pruner, but leave limbs high in the canopy to a professional with the proper equipment.*

## Feed the Trees

Feed newly planted trees with a fertilizer that contains slow-release nitrogen. There are many brands of tree-and-shrub food containing slow-release fertilizer, with formulas that vary from 12-6-6 to 18-18-18. Because each is formulated a little differently, *be sure* to apply it at the rate recommended on the label.

If you do not have a slow-release tree-and-shrub food, you may fertilize a newly planted tree with 5-10-10 or a similar formula that is low in nitrogen and high in phosphorus. Apply about ½ to 1 cup per tree. Older, established trees do not need to be regularly fertilized—they receive all the nutrients they need through your regular lawn-fertilization program.

## How and When To Apply

The easiest way to apply fertilizer is to scatter it over the outside edges of the planting hole and the soil around it. While spring feeding is typical, trees benefit from a fall feeding immediately after the first killing frost. Feeding after frost with a formula low in nitrogen, such as 5-10-10 or a "winterizer" product, will still deliver nutrients to the roots without enticing new growth that could be damaged by freezing temperatures.

# Pruning

Most trees need little if any pruning. Generally, the only reasons to prune are to thin the crown, to remove dead wood or awkward branches, or to shape the tree. Exceptions are crabapples and weeping willows, two excessively branched trees, and crape myrtles, which flower better with a little tip pruning.

If you cannot safely make the pruning cuts that you need with a pole pruner or a pruning saw, hire a bonded and insured tree service to do the work. Climbing into a tree may be hazardous to you or to others on the ground.

## Thinning the Canopy

Thinning means removing branches from the interior of the tree's crown to permit air and light to penetrate. This reduces the likelihood of disease, such as sooty mold. In areas prone to hurricanes or other violent storms, thinning reduces pressure on the tree by allowing strong winds to blow through it. Also, if you are training a small tree to assume a specific form, thinning the canopy speeds growth by preventing the waste of resources on superfluous branches.

## Removing Dead Wood

Dead branches can harbor harmful insects, may be sources of disease, or could fall on someone or something below. Timely pruning may avert the spread of decay or disease into the heart of the tree. Cut the branch back to healthy wood or, if the entire limb is dead, to the outer edge of the *collar,* the swollen base where the branch joins the trunk.

## Awkward Branching

Prune any annoying branches, such as those you must dodge, those that slap the house during a windstorm, or those growing contrary to the normal branching pattern of the tree. Branches that crisscross in the tree's interior may eventually rub together, causing open sores that welcome diseases and insects. This is often the case with crape myrtles and crabapples.

## Shaping for Special Effect

Some trees need to be shaped to maintain particular designs within the landscape. Crape myrtles need tip pruning each winter to encourage flowering. A sheared hemlock hedge requires annual attention; prune these plants before new growth starts in the spring. Be sure to keep the bottom of the sheared hedge wider than the top to prevent the lower part from being shaded out.

Some trees, such as sycamore, may be trimmed back so that they produce dense clusters of foliage on short branches. This technique, called *pollarding,* needs to be done in fall, after the leaves drop.

*Espaliered* trees, those that are trained to grow against a flat support, require constant attention to maintain the geometry of their intent. This involves the removal of wayward branches and the fastening of new growth to the surface. In spring, make cuts just as new growth begins, to direct the plant's energy in the preferred direction. Follow up in fall to remove other errant shoots.

## A WORD ABOUT PRUNING SAWS AND POLE PRUNERS

The size of the branch determines whether you need shears or a saw. For small branches (1½ inches or less in diameter), pruning shears or lopping shears will be adequate. The best shears have two cutting edges and work like scissors. Larger branches require the serrated blade of a pruning saw.

A pole pruner can extend your reach and will allow you to prune higher branches safely. It is a long pole with a metal hook at the top. Within the hook is a sharp pruning blade that is levered by a cord. When you pull the cord, the blade will cut the branch, which is held by the hook. These pole pruners work best for cutting branches that are 1 inch or less in diameter.

Consider a pole pruner with a top-mounted saw blade, an extension that will allow you to cut branches up to 3 inches in diameter. Metal telescoping pole pruners are the most adaptable, but take extra precautions when working around the power lines that serve your home.

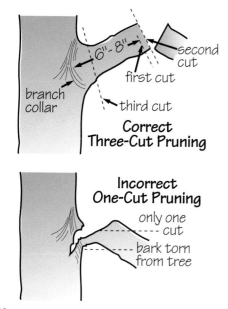

*If you must remove a limb or branches, use the proper method to prevent damage.*

*To avoid harming existing trees, build decking around them rather than grading around the root zone for a walkway or a terrace.*

## Proper Cuts Critical to Tree Health

Do not make pruning cuts flush with the trunk of the tree. Instead, cut branches back only as far as the collar. The collar appears as a knob of concentric rings of bark forming a protective barrier against diseases and insects. Even after you remove the branch, the collar will continue to grow, sealing the cut.

Pruning a branch correctly leaves a wound that is roughly circular in shape. To produce this, you will have to make three cuts for each branch you remove. Make the first cut on the underside of the branch, approximately 6 to 8 inches out from the collar. Cut about one-fourth of the way through. Make the second cut on the top side, slightly farther out than the undercut, cutting through the branch. Because of your first protective cut, the branch will fall without tearing away any bark.

Finally, cut the remaining branch back to the collar; do not leave a stub beyond the collar. Unless the tree is an oak, you do not need to paint the cut with tree paint.

## Protecting Trees

It takes at least three years for a tree to reveal the extent of damage suffered during nearby construction. Protecting trees during construction is one of the most difficult and possibly most expensive tasks you can undertake.

The solution is very simple: do not disturb the feeding area of the roots. Avoid driving or parking construction equipment or storing dirt, bricks, or other materials under the tree. The added weight above the roots compacts the soil, crushing or tearing feeder roots and impairing the tree's ability to absorb both nutrients and oxygen. If no equipment enters the tree's feeding area, which extends well beyond the edge of the canopy, there is little possibility of hitting the trunk and tearing the bark.

Also avoid grading in the root zone. Construction is followed by rough grading for drainage and fine grading for a lawn, both extremely damaging to previously undisturbed root systems. The damage to the roots results in the gradual death of the crown, which may occur over a period of three years.

The only way to guarantee that a tree will not be damaged is to keep offending materials and equipment away from the tree. Typically, a tree can withstand the removal of one-third of its feeding area. Some trees, such as pines and hickories, seem more tolerant of root encroachment; others, especially dogwoods and American beeches, are very sensitive to this invasion.

It is possible to raise the level of the grade around a tree without killing it, but such construction is expensive. Any fill material should begin with a layer of coarse gravel, which permits air to reach the feeder roots. Then a series of pipes must be installed to provide air and watering access to the root system after the final filling. Since circumstances will vary, it is best to consult an arborist or a landscape architect about the problem in order to design the necessary measures.

## LAWN MOWERS ARE A TREE'S WORST ENEMY

A tree's bark is like your skin, the first line of defense against infection. Unfortunately, nicking the bark with a lawn mower can open the tree up to possible diseases. Young trees are particularly vulnerable because their bark is thin.

You can protect newly planted trees in one of two ways. Wrap a purchased tree wrap or a split section of PVC pipe around the trunk. Or spread a 4-foot circle of mulch around the tree to prevent anyone from mowing too close to the trunk.

*A bed of mulch ties together existing pines and keeps mowers and string trimmers away from their bases.*

# Plant Hardiness Zone Map

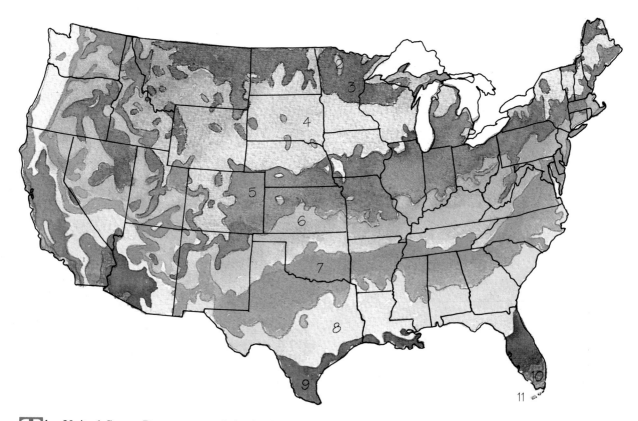

The United States Department of Agriculture has charted low temperatures throughout the country to determine the ranges of average low readings. The map above is based loosely on the USDA Plant Hardiness Zone Map, which was drawn from these findings. It does not take into account heat, soil, or moisture extremes and is intended as a guide, not a guarantee.

The southern regions of the United States that are mentioned in this book refer to the following:

**Upper South:** Zone 6

**Middle South:** upper region of Zone 7 (0 to 5 degrees minimum)

**Lower South:** lower region of Zone 7 and upper region of Zone 8 (5 to 15 degrees minimum)

**Coastal South:** lower region of Zone 8 and upper region of Zone 9 (15 to 25 degrees minimum)

**Tropical South:** lower region of Zone 9 and all of Zone 10 (25 to 40 degrees minimum)

| Zone 2 | -50 | to | -40°F |
|---|---|---|---|
| Zone 3 | -40 | to | -30°F |
| Zone 4 | -30 | to | -20°F |
| Zone 5 | -20 | to | -10°F |
| Zone 6 | -10 | to | 0°F |
| Zone 7 | 0 | to | 10°F |
| Zone 8 | 10 | to | 20°F |
| Zone 9 | 20 | to | 30°F |
| Zone 10 | 30 | to | 40°F |
| Zone 11 | | above | 40°F |

# Tree Profiles

The trees described in the following pages were selected by the garden editors at *Southern Living* for their availability, dependability, and many garden uses, which make them the most popular and reliable trees for successful landscaping. You will find most of these trees for sale at garden centers, but some are native trees that you may find already thriving on your property.

Arranged alphabetically by common name, these profiles give you a description of each tree and the different selections that you will see for sale, information about planting and care, and suggested ways that you can incorporate its color, height, and form into your garden. Critical to your success is knowing the soil and cultural conditions each tree needs; this information, as well as troubleshooting tips and techniques, is contained in the profiles.

When a family of trees, such as the maples, includes more than one species, the group is discussed in a single entry. The profile points out the differences in appearance and growing needs of the most popular trees within the group.

For a quick overview of the tree, refer to the *At a Glance* box that accompanies every profile. This will give you the major features of the tree, including its botanical name to help you avoid confusion when buying trees to plant.

Trees are important elements in the landscape. Their successful growth depends upon your care and maintenance; with proper care, the right trees can shade and shield your home for generations.

*Crape myrtle*

*Sugar maples*

# Bald Cypress

*Soft, needlelike leaves give bald cypress a fine texture.*

Native to Southern swamps, bald cypress seems an unlikely tree for landscape use. However, it is a perfect choice because of its appearance and its adaptability to both wet and dry soils. This tree is tolerant of soils that are low in oxygen and is a surprisingly good choice for street plantings, where root space is often constricted and the soil may be compacted.

## A Closer Look

Bald cypress grows quickly into an almost perfect cone shape. You can expect a 7-foot cypress to reach 20 feet in height in 10 to 15 years, but it will never have a broad crown. Mature trees, reaching 50 to 70 feet, rarely have a spread of more than 30 feet. In the wild, trees form a wide trunk base and roots above the ground, or "knees"; these modifications for wet conditions will not appear unless you plant bald cypress near water.

Bald cypress has the needles typical of conifers, but unlike most conifers it is deciduous. The tree has a soft outline that is enhanced by its delicate, featherlike foliage and casts only a light shade, permitting lawn grasses to grow. In fall, the pliable, light green needles turn a golden brown, covering the ground below to create a beautiful carpet. In winter, the bare branches are decorated with brown cones that are about an inch in diameter but are rarely numerous enough to create a litter problem.

*Fall shows off the color changes of a cypress tree.*

## In the Landscape

Because bald cypress shows high tolerance for very poor soils, it can be planted as a street tree or around newly constructed homes. Use it as a specimen tree at the junction of a driveway and the street or to symmetrically line a driveway. This tree does not drop fruit, making it a good choice to plant near a patio, and the narrow crown makes it suitable for foundation plantings. Be sure to plant bald cypress at least 15 feet from the house.

### AT A GLANCE
❖
### BALD CYPRESS
*Taxodium distichum*

**Features:** beautiful foliage, reddish bark

**Foliage:** deciduous

**Outstanding season:** spring

**Height:** 50 to 70 feet

**Spread:** 20 to 30 feet

**Growth rate:** medium

**Native:** yes

**Range:** Zones 4 to 9

**Light:** full sun

**Pests:** none specific

**Remarks:** grows in wet or dry soil

*In urban conditions, bald cypress will thrive as a street tree.*

*Bald cypress, native to Southern wetlands, is adaptable to landscapes with wet or dry soil.*

Landscape designers often plant these trees in groups of three and position them in a triangle to enhance the tree's conical form. Trees planted this way are especially nice when viewed across the smooth surface of a pond. Properties with a sunny creek or other wet areas also welcome a bald cypress.

## Planting and Care

Bald cypress grows best in deep sandy loam with plenty of moisture, but it is also tolerant of heavy clay. Young plants grow very rapidly, particularly if they are planted near a source of water, such as a lake or a streambed or the drip from an air-conditioning system. These trees are also tolerant of dry soil once their roots are well established.

## Different Selections

Most bald cypress seedlings are labeled simply bald cypress; there are few named selections.

Pond cypress *(Taxodium ascendens)* is another native species that is more columnar and less wide than bald cypress, although mature specimens in the wild may be more irregular in form than bald cypress. The needles lie close along the branches and are not as feathery as those of bald cypress. Bald cypress and pond cypress may be distinguished by the way the branches layer; those of pond cypress have an ascending form. The use and range of adaptability of pond cypress are the same as bald cypress.

**41**

# Beech

*The parchment-colored leaves last all winter until new growth appears in the spring.*

American beech is a native shade tree that is outstanding in every season. After the lime green foliage emerges from brown, cigar-shaped buds in spring, the tree settles into the role of a handsome, deep green shade tree. In autumn, the leaves turn an exquisite golden bronze, a color no other tree duplicates. In late fall, the foliage gradually changes to a warm parchment color and then to deep brown. American beech's smooth, light gray bark is revealed in winter, and the leaves often flutter until spring. On rainy or foggy days moisture causes these curled leaves to open up and brighten an otherwise somber landscape.

## A Closer Look

American beech slowly grows into a large tree, typically 50 to 70 feet in height (sometimes 100 feet in the wild) with a spread of 40 to 60 feet. Branches bear silvery-gray twigs that are finely textured and angled in a zigzag pattern. Leaves vary from 2 to 5 inches in length and are dark glossy green on top and slightly lighter underneath.

The fruit—the edible beechnut—is enclosed in a prickly four-sided capsule. It is a favorite food of many birds, including titmice, jays, and grosbeaks, as well as squirrels and other animals; therefore, it seldom remains on the ground. The tree will invariably have a nest high in its branches.

## In the Landscape

To enjoy American beech to the fullest, plant it near your favorite window to view the effect of the leaves in winter. This tree can serve as an open-lawn specimen at the end of a garden vista or may be set in a border. You may want to use a beech as the feature tree beside a driveway because its high branching structure is easy to walk or drive

---

### AT A GLANCE

#### BEECH
*Fagus grandifolia*

**Features:** beautiful form, foliage, and bark

**Foliage:** deciduous

**Outstanding season:** all seasons

**Height:** 50 to 70 feet

**Spread:** 40 to 60 feet

**Growth rate:** slow to moderate

**Native:** yes

**Range:** Zones 3 to 9

**Light:** full sun to partial shade

**Pests:** none specific

**Remarks:** one of the most stately native trees

beneath. It is also stunning when planted with other beech trees in a grove. Because of American beech's dense foliage and many shallow roots, you should plant only vigorous, shade-tolerant ground covers beneath these trees.

Take advantage of the silvery-gray bark. Silhouette American beech against a wall or outbuilding, such as a garage. The bark and winter leaves are also elegant when poised against an evergreen backdrop, such as white pine or hemlock.

If you are building a home on a lot with tall trees, use a young beech for accent by planting it beneath the existing canopy of trees. This duplicates the natural circumstances under which beech trees thrive and in winter will introduce the wonderful effects of the deep brown leaves into the garden.

# Planting and Care

American beech must have moist but well-drained acid soil that is rich in organic matter (such as that used for rhododendrons or azaleas). The tree will not grow in compacted soil, heavy clay, or soils that are perpetually wet. It does best in full sun but will live quite well in an opening amid taller trees. Place it at least 20 feet from the house to give it room to spread.

American beech develops a dense network of hairlike roots just below the surface of the soil, making it extremely difficult to grow lawn grasses beneath the canopy. In fact, a shade-loving ground cover or no planting at all is the best treatment under these trees.

If you build or remodel near existing beeches, you must keep construction equipment beyond the canopy of the trees, as beeches are sensitive to soil compaction and are likely to suffer root damage.

# Different Selections

Most beech trees are sold simply as American beech with few hybrid or named selections available.

European beech *(Fagus sylvatica)* is just as magnificent as its native counterpart, but it grows best in Zones 4 to 7. Two of many fine selections include Atropunicea, also known as Purpurea, a stunning specimen with purple leaves, and the weeping beech, Pendula, which retains its mesmerizing pendulous form even in winter.

*These beech trees shade a driveway and create a stately entry to this residence.*

*Young American beech trees splash spots of warm color against the more somber palette of gray in winter.*

# Birch

*Heritage river birch is valued for its light-colored bark and is very ornamental during winter.*

The natural versatility of river birch has taken it beyond its native home along streams and lowlands of the Eastern United States and into gardens of all elevations. A fast-growing tree, river birch can thrive in wet or dry soil. This fast growth and easy culture has made it a landscape staple.

## A Closer Look

River birch delivers a light, airy shade and features wonderfully shaggy, multicolored bark and an upright growth habit. Lacking showy flowers or fall color, this native tree relies on its bark for landscape appeal. Beige paperlike sheets peel back to reveal darker layers of bark. The result is year-round beauty; it is especially fine in winter, when much of the landscape is bare.

The tree's slender, twiggy branches give it an airy, breezy appearance. The branches are thinner than those of other trees and tend to droop under their own weight, giving the tree a pendulous look. In spring, river birch bears delicate *catkins,* long, stringy flowers without petals. The foliage has medium to fine texture and is grass green, turning an uninspired yellow in fall.

## In the Landscape

Use river birch beside your deck or patio. Give it plenty of water in summer and you will have light shade in just a few years.

The bark makes river birch an excellent tree to plant near walkways; however, bear in mind that it is a large tree, growing to 70 feet or more. The canopy is thin enough to allow grass to grow beneath it, so you can use it freely in an open lawn. Or, plant river birches in a grove and mass ground cover and flowering bulbs beneath the trees.

River birch has an architectural quality that makes it a good choice for a foundation planting. If you plant it near the corner of a two-story house, place it at least 20 feet from the foundation to permit healthy root development around the tree. If you use river birch to provide shade over a paved area, allow plenty of room for the roots to develop. This will keep the tree in top health and will reduce the dropping of twigs, which a struggling river birch will tend to do. However, even trees in the best of health will drop some twigs and leaves so expect to rake or sweep occasionally.

## AT A GLANCE

❖

### RIVER BIRCH
*Betula nigra*

**Features:** outstanding bark
**Foliage:** deciduous
**Outstanding season:** summer, winter
**Height:** 40 to 70 feet
**Spread:** 40 to 60 feet
**Growth rate:** rapid
**Native:** yes
**Range:** Zones 4 to 9
**Light:** full sun
**Pests:** aphids
**Remarks:** best birch for the South

## Planting and Care

River birch prefers a location in full sun to one with partial shade. Although it is tolerant of dry soil, it will grow best in moist or even soggy sites. Water it during periods of dry weather and it will reward you with 3 feet of annual growth. River birch does not tolerate alkaline soil; it must have acid soil or the leaves will turn a sickly yellow.

## Different Selections

Heritage has lighter colored bark than the species and is often selected for its heavy peeling. Its large, dark green leaves have a leathery texture.

## Troubleshooting

Fortunately, river birch has few pests or diseases compared to other birches. Aphids are the worst pest; the area under infested trees will be sprinkled with honeydew, a sugary, sticky secretion. See page 124 for more about aphids.

*River birch will grow especially fast if given lots of water.*

# Bradford Pear

*Bradford pear's brilliant foliage makes it as spectacular in fall as it is in spring.*

Few trees offer the showy spring flowers and formal growth habit of Bradford pear. In fall, its leaves turn deep crimson and are rivaled by few other trees. This ornamental tree tolerates drought, heat, and poor soil while growing very fast—up to 3 feet a year. However, Bradford pear may not be the perfect tree for the home landscape because it splits easily, especially in stormy weather.

## A Closer Look

Bradford pear has an upright, rounded form. When first introduced, this tree was touted as an ideal small deciduous ornamental. Time has shown that this stellar small tree is not so small after all—it easily grows from 30 to 50 feet high with a spread of 20 to 35 feet.

Bradford pear's white flowers are borne in clusters in early spring, usually before the leaves begin to unfurl. Small russet-colored fruit follows the flowers and is often eaten by birds before it falls to the ground. (This fruit is inedible to humans.)

Part of the tree's summer appeal is its lustrous, deep green foliage. The individual leaves are about 3 inches long and nearly heart shaped. Bradford pear's leaves make a stunning transition to fall, burning orange then crimson before dropping. The upward branching habit, paired with the tree's dark gray bark, retains the formal appeal of the tree during the winter.

### AT A GLANCE
❖
### BRADFORD PEAR
*Pyrus calleryana* Bradford

**Features:** outstanding flowers, form, and fall color

**Foliage:** deciduous

**Outstanding season:** spring, fall

**Height:** 30 to 50 feet

**Spread:** 20 to 35 feet

**Growth rate:** rapid

**Native:** no

**Range:** Zones 4 to 8

**Light:** full sun

**Pests:** fire blight

**Remarks:** considered a short-lived tree

*Bradford pear produces dependable spring blooms.*

# In the Landscape

Bradford pear works best in settings that call for a formal tree. It is a good choice to shade a terrace; use it as a feature tree in a shrub border or the corner of a formal garden. This tree also works well along a driveway or in a circular driveway directly in front of the house. A pair of these trees can dress up the space between the driveway and the property line.

Bradford pear needs plenty of room to grow. When using the tree as an open-lawn specimen, plant it at least 15 feet from the house. The dense branching and foliage make these trees a good summer screen.

# Planting and Care

You may plant Bradford pear in full sun and any soil that drains well. The tree will flourish in heavy clay or sand and in urban conditions.

# Troubleshooting

Ironically, Bradford pear's tidy branching habit is its landscape downfall—the tree's sharp, angular branching structure makes it subject to devastating wind and ice damage. A strong wind may snap off the top half of the branches, and ice can literally split the tree.

Because of these problems, many growers are phasing out Bradford pear in favor of newer, improved selections. These new trees have the same showy spring flowers but lack some of Bradford pear's dependable fall color. However, corrective pruning can thwart ice and wind damage to Bradford pear. Over a three-year period, remove about one-third of the main limbs, concentrating on those that form the V-shaped crotch at the trunk.

Bradford pear is susceptible to fire blight, a bacterial disease that causes the leaves and twigs to die back. Control fire blight by spraying early in the spring while the tree is in bloom, as the bacteria is spread by bees visiting the flowers. Newer selections are less suspectible to fire blight.

*The branching habit of Bradford pear is responsible for its lollipop shape but also makes it subject to splitting in storms.*

# Different Selections

Aristocrat grows to the same size as Bradford but is more rounded and has stronger branching joints. Chanticleer has an upright, pyramidal form that is more narrow than Bradford and better suited to tight locations. Paradise develops into a beautiful small tree, only 20 feet tall and 15 feet wide.

# Cherry

*Yoshino cherry blossoms open from pink buds and then quickly fade to white.*

The flowering cherries start spring with just a sprinkle of fragile blossoms and then become covered in pastel color seemingly overnight. For about ten days each spring, they bloom as though this season might be their last, making a memorable show wherever they are planted.

Because of their small stature, cherry trees are typically used as accent trees in a lawn, near a favorite window, or at the edge of a terrace or a deck. While none are extremely long-lived, Japanese flowering cherry, Taiwan cherry, and the sturdy hybrid Yoshino cherry usually live a decade or two. Higan cherry often lives 30 years or more.

## A Closer Look

The blossoms of flowering cherries vary in color from deep pink to white. Individual blossoms may be single or double and are arranged in clusters of four or five. The inconspicuous fruit that follows the flowers of ornamental cherries is seldom visible and is not edible.

Cherry foliage is deep green and tapered with serrated edges. In some selections, most noticeably Kwanzan, the young leaves have bronze highlights when they first appear in spring.

Flowering cherries have a medium texture and are quite handsome in summer. They cast a heavy to mottled shade, depending on how densely the canopy has grown (the more sun, the more dense the tree). In autumn, the leaves turn orange red. When the leaves fall, a finely branched but very appealing profile is revealed. Cherry bark is characteristically shiny and scored with horizontal *lenticels,* scarlike markings through which the tree "breathes."

## In the Landscape

With the exception of the weeping types, flowering cherries form a vase-shaped canopy that has a wide, slightly flattened crown. This makes cherries good understory trees on a large lot. Use a cherry tree in an architectural setting as a shade tree for a patio or as the featured

### AT A GLANCE

❖

### CHERRY
*Prunus species*

**Features:** exquisite flowers and bark

**Foliage:** deciduous

**Outstanding season:** spring

**Height:** 15 to 50 feet

**Spread:** 15 to 30 feet

**Growth rate:** rapid

**Native:** no

**Range:** Zones 5 to 9

**Light:** full sun to partial shade

**Pests:** borers

**Remarks:** not a long-lived tree

*A matched pair of Yoshino cherries offers light shade and ornamental qualities.*

tree along a garden walkway. Cherries work best as accents in more formal gardens—as feature trees in a parterre garden, for example—or in other gardens where strong design organization is needed.

Cherries also make excellent single specimens beside a driveway or as the feature tree in a small garden. They are exceptionally lovely around fountains or ponds where their blossoms are reflected in the water.

Cherries work well as a mass planting; three or four planted together around a bed of ground cover can help create a space in the landscape. Flowering cherries make excellent lawn specimens, particularly individual trees that have branches very close to the ground. Because they have a vigorous root system, it is best to plan for a ground cover beneath the trees or let them branch to the ground.

*The bark of a cherry tree is scored with horizontal markings.*

*Weeping cherry is a fountain of flowers in early spring before the leaves appear.*

Weeping cherries offer a different landscape use. Because of their unusual form, they are visually dominating and need center stage; plant one as the central feature of an herb garden or as an accent tree near a patio or a terrace.

## Planting and Care

You may plant cherries in full sun or partial shade, although plants in sun will flower more profusely. They need acid soil that is moist but well drained and rich in organic matter. Cherries grow rapidly, provided they are watered and fertilized well. Under good conditions, trees can grow up to 3 feet a year.

## Species and Selections

Selections of Higan cherry *(Prunus subhirtella)* include Autumnalis, which blooms in pink in fall, winter, and early spring. Pendula is the weeping Higan cherry and has soft pink single flowers that appear before the leaves.

Japanese flowering cherry *(Prunus serrulata)* selections include the showy Kwanzan (also called Sekiyama), which has profuse rose-pink double flowers and slightly bronze young foliage. Shirofugen bears large (2½-inch) pink double flowers that fade to pure white. Mt. Fuji, also called Shirotae cherry, bears large double flowers in white.

Yoshino cherry *(Prunus x yedoensis)* is the famous flowering cherry of Washington, D.C. It is also the largest of the flowering cherries, growing as tall as 50 feet.

Most cherries look best in spring following a cold winter; Taiwan cherry *(Prunus campanulata)* is more tolerant of the mild winters of the lower South. It is not as cold hardy as other cherries, generally growing only in Zones 7 to 9. Taiwan cherry has dark pink blossoms that appear in late winter or early spring. It is among the smallest cherries, growing 15 to 20 feet high. Okame is a selection with showy red twigs.

## Troubleshooting

Cherries are often bothered by borers, which may cause the limbs to die back. Sometimes the whole tree will be affected. See page 124 for more about borers.

*Kwanzan cherry is prized for its double blooms.*

# Crabapple

Crabapple is unmatched among flowering trees for its two distinct shows. In spring it blooms after the flowering cherries and before the dogwoods, becoming a fountain of color in white, pink, or vivid red. The flowers are so thick that they block your view through the tree. Then the flowers mature into fruits, and the tree is covered with vivid ornaments during late summer and fall.

## A Closer Look

The crabapple is aptly named, as it is covered in small, red, applelike fruit. Technically only the size of the fruit distinguishes an apple from a crabapple; fruit greater than 2 inches in diameter is an apple, and anything less is a crabapple. However, apples for fresh eating have better flavor than crabapples.

The small crabapples are especially prominent when the tree is planted against a backdrop of green foliage or a wall. The fruit is an outstanding garden feature as it often remains on the branches long after the leaves have fallen. In winter, the tree has a distinctive twiggy form and may hold on to a few persistent fruit. It also has a deep gray bark that exfoliates in patches on older trees.

## In the Landscape

Crabapples easily grow to 20 feet high and 25 feet wide. They look best either grouped in a drift in the foreground of taller trees or used as single specimens in a bed of ground cover, into which the fruit may drop. Plant at the crown of a hill so you may see the cloudlike bloom silhouetted against the sky, or place the tree in front of an evergreen hedge. Crabapple makes a fine lawn specimen if you keep it pruned and cleaned of *suckers,* thin shoots that sprout from the trunk and interior branches.

Most crabapples have a mounding form and very dense foliage. Use their mass to visually break a large expanse of masonry or siding, such as the side of a garage. While most crabapples are too large for a garden border, a notable exception is Sargent crabapple, a dwarf species that is both handsome and small enough for a townhouse courtyard; be sure to leave plenty of room for the fruit to drop.

Crabapple can be an effective deciduous screen; its branching habit is thick enough to partially obscure undesirable views even in winter. The fruit attracts birds and the thick branches are the perfect place for nests.

*Crabapple is named for the applelike fruit it bears in late summer and fall.*

### AT A GLANCE
### CRABAPPLE
*Malus species and hybrids*

**Features:** white, red, or pink flowers; bright red fruit

**Foliage:** deciduous

**Outstanding season:** spring, summer, fall

**Height:** 8 to 40 feet

**Spread:** 10 to 40 feet

**Growth rate:** moderate to rapid

**Native:** some

**Range:** Zones 4 to 8

**Light:** full sun

**Pests:** apple scab, fire blight, cedar-apple rust

**Remarks:** excellent fall show

*Crabapple trees are dense with blooms in spring.*

*A close look reveals delicate flowers so profuse that their stems are nearly concealed.*

## Planting and Care

Crabapple prefers moist, well-drained soil that is slightly acid. The tree also needs full sun for best flowering and fruit production. Suckers often sprout from the trunk and branches, leading to a tangle of criss-crossing branches. To shape the tree, be sure to prune new shoots by late spring, as buds for next year's blossoms form in summer.

## Species and Selections

There are several hundred crabapple selections available. Before you buy, check with a local garden source for selections that may be particularly suited to your climate, as they vary greatly in cold hardiness, heat tolerance, and resistance to disease. See the chart on page 53 for a list of superior selections. The crabapples discussed below do well throughout the Mid-Atlantic and Southern states.

Callaway crabapple (*Malus* Callaway) is an upright tree that bears white flowers and grows 15 to 20 feet high. It is known for its disease resistance and its ability to withstand the hot, humid conditions of the lower South. Dolgo (*Malus* Dolgo) is a large hybrid tree that grows to 40 feet in height with large fruit that is popular for making jellies.

Japanese flowering crabapple *(Malus floribunda)* grows 15 to 20 feet tall. Its buds are deep pink to red and produce single white flowers with a pink blush. The fragrant blooms are followed by red-and-yellow fruit. Sargent crabapple *(Malus sargentii)* is a dwarf crabapple, growing only 6 to 8 feet tall but very wide, like a large, mounded shrub. It has single white flowers and bright red fruit.

You may see Southern crabapple *(Malus angustifolia)* growing in the wild, as it is native to the South. However, this tree is susceptible to fire blight, so other selections are better suited to the garden.

## Troubleshooting

Three diseases, apple scab, fire blight, and cedar-apple rust, can turn a crabapple from a flowering show into a landscape blemish. To avoid these problems choose a selection that is resistant.

Apple scab causes dull, smoky spots to appear on the leaves and usually results in heavy leaf drop. The fruits also develop rough black spots. It looks terrible, but will not seriously injure the tree.

Fire blight can kill a crabapple. The disease causes the leaves, the flowers, and the branches to look as though they have been scorched by fire. The leaves wilt and then suddenly turn black and die.

This is a bacterial disease that causes the leaves and twigs to die back; it appears sporadically in different parts of the tree. You can control fire blight by spraying in early spring while the trees are in bloom, as the bacteria is often spread by bees visiting the flowers. Contact your county Extension agent for a recommended spray.

Cedar-apple rust produces orange spots on the leaves, and then the leaves drop. This disease needs the cohost of red cedar and is generally not a problem if cedar trees are not grown in the area.

## DEGREE OF DISEASE RESISTANCE

| Selection | Apple Scab | Fire Blight | Cedar-Apple Rust |
|---|---|---|---|
| Adams | Good | Excellent | Excellent |
| Adirondack | Excellent | Excellent | Excellent |
| Baskatong | Good | Excellent | Excellent |
| Callaway | Excellent | Good | Good |
| Candied Apple | Good | Good | Good |
| Centurion | Good | Excellent | Excellent |
| Dolgo | Good | Good | Excellent |
| Eleyi | Very Poor | Fair | Fair |
| Hopa | Very Poor | Fair | Fair |
| Indian Summer | Good | Excellent | Excellent |
| Japanese flowering | Good | Fair | Excellent |
| Katherine | Good | Good | Good |
| Liset | Excellent | Good | Excellent |
| Prairifire | Excellent | Excellent | Excellent |
| Professor Sprenger | Excellent | Excellent | Excellent |
| Radiant | Poor | Good | Good |
| Red Jewel | Fair | Fair | Excellent |
| Robinson | Good | Excellent | Excellent |
| Sargent | Excellent | Good | Excellent |
| Snowdrift | Good | Poor | Excellent |
| Strawberry Parfait | Good | Fair | Good |
| White Cascade | Good | Excellent | Excellent |
| Zumi | Good | Poor | Excellent |

*Crabapple fruit may be so small that they appear to be large berries.*

# Crape Myrtle

*Crape myrtle is named for its soft, crapelike blooms.*

Crape myrtle, the premier tree for summer flowers in the South, salutes the heat with a colorful display. But the summer show is just one of crape myrtle's highlights. Handsome bark is a year-round attribute, and its bright fall color is hard to beat. These qualities, combined with its manageable stature and iron-clad dependability, keep crape myrtle high on the list of delightfully rewarding small trees.

## A Closer Look

Crape myrtle blooms are actually a cluster of flowers in a *panicle*, a loosely branched cluster. The flowers do not all open at the same time, so the period of bloom lasts a month or more. The panicles are from 6 to 12 inches long and between 4 and 7 inches wide; they are so heavy on the tree that they bend the branches in a graceful weeping habit. Colors include white, various shades of pinks, reds, and lavenders, and bicolored combinations.

In summer, the thin, paperlike bark peels away to reveal a smooth trunk and branches in colors ranging from tan to gray to cinnamon brown, depending on the selection. In winter, the bare trunk and branches provide a sculptural silhouette.

Crape myrtle is one of the most dependable trees for fall color in the lower and coastal South. Leaves turn a brilliant gold, orange, or red; sometimes all three colors appear on a single tree.

## In the Landscape

Crape myrtle is available in many heights and is suited to various uses in the landscape. Medium-sized trees reach 12 to 20 feet tall. Large selections may grow to 20 feet tall or more and at least 10 feet wide, making a good small canopy for shade. Most are small enough for planting beneath power lines. Crape myrtle may be planted as a live "fence" across a back property line. This tree does well where room for either the roots or the crown is restricted.

Consider medium-sized and large crape myrtles to shade a patio, a terrace, or a low deck. Single specimens may be used as the feature tree in a courtyard or a small garden, at the corner of a sidewalk and the street, or in the curve of a driveway.

Crape myrtle trees are usually shaped with three or more trunks; this multitrunked form, which is strongly architectural in character, is outstanding along a sidewalk or in repetition across a solid background such as a wall, a fence, an evergreen screen, or the front of a house. Because of its bark and form, crape myrtle looks impressive when silhouetted against a stone wall or a wooden fence.

*Crape myrtle easily grows in the narrow strip between the curb and the sidewalk and will not interfere with overhead power lines.*

Paired trees work well on either side of a driveway or on opposite sides of an entry; plant each tree at least 6 feet from the house. Trees planted in multiples are very useful in narrow side yards or in beds of ground cover.

Dwarf crape myrtles are not really trees. Only 3 feet tall, they are popular as ground covers and for baskets and pots. Semidwarf selections grow from 3 to 6 feet in height; they are used as small shrubs and are also popular for large pots.

## Planting and Care

Crape myrtle will grow best in rich, moist soil, although it will tolerate any soil that drains well. Crape myrtle will even tolerate the alkaline soils of Texas, Oklahoma, and Arkansas. However, crape myrtle demands full sun; shade is often a reason for poor blooming.

Light pruning will help crape myrtle retain a nice form and will increase blooming. Tip pruning, or snipping off the flower clusters as they fade in late summer, will encourage established trees to bloom again in fall. The spent flowers are followed by round fruit capsules that will remain on the tree through winter. Tip-prune again in late

*Crape myrtle is a perfect size for planting near the house.*

**55**

winter to remove the capsules and encourage the growth of more flowering stems.

Often you will see trees cut back drastically along the trunk. This results in a tangle of growth just above the cuts and an abnormal, gnarly look. Stems that you trim back to encourage branching and flowering should be no thicker than a pencil.

You should also remove shoots that arise from the base of the tree or along the trunks. Cut these off at the point of origin. This keeps the trunks clean and enhances the tree's drama.

## Different Selections

Many hybrid crape myrtles offer resistance to powdery mildew as well as exceptional bark and flower color. Catawba has dark purple flowers with a compact form. Cherokee has brilliant red blooms and an open, spreading habit. Conestoga offers lavender flowers and an open growth habit. Potomac is a medium pink and blooms for a long time. Powhatan has light purple flowers and a compact growth

*The sculptural form of the bark and trunks gives crape myrtle a unique winter signature.*

*In summer, a small crape myrtle extends the screening effect of this garden wall.*

*A cluster of crape myrtles can provide privacy in spring and summer.*

habit. Seminole has medium pink blooms and a short, upright habit. Natchez is a white-flowered selection with exceptional cinnamon-colored bark; give it room, as it grows 20 to 25 feet tall.

## Troubleshooting

Although crape myrtles are long-lived, durable, and tolerant of many conditions, they are troubled by a few pests. Aphids will appear with the tender growth in spring, but they disappear when temperatures reach 90 degrees. However, if aphids are feeding as the flower buds form, they may do so much damage that the tree will not bloom. Turn to page 124 for more about aphids.

Sooty mold, a black fungus, grows on the aphid secretions. It does not hurt the tree and will disappear as you get rid of the aphids.

Powdery mildew may attack the leaves of older selections and cause the foliage to yellow or drop. To avoid this, plant mildew-resistant selections, such as Catawba, Natchez, Cherokee, Muskogee, Powhatan, Seminole, or Tuscarora. Turn to page 125 to read more about powdery mildew.

Crape myrtle roots are not large, but are very competitive; it can be difficult to grow other plants beneath the trees. Choose sturdy ground covers that can compete, such as mondo grass, liriope, or Asian jasmine.

*Fall color is brilliant, even in the lower South where fall foliage is generally muted.*

# Dogwood

*The four unfolding "petals" of the flowering dogwood are not petals at all, but bracts. They surround the true flowers—the small yellow ones in the center.*

No other tree can bring the woodlands alive like a dogwood. The unfolding blossoms of this native understory tree dot the landscape with airy drifts of white (and sometimes pink) that look like clouds amidst the trunks of taller trees. Every dogwood is different; no two trees will ever look exactly alike because the tree's form is the result of its reach for sunlight in the shady understory of its natural habitat.

## A Closer Look

Dogwoods growing in shade have an open look; the branches grow in a strong pattern of horizontal layers with open gaps between. The 3- to 6-inch-long leaves are a soft, light green, contrasting with the often deeper color of pines and other canopy trees overhead.

Although the flowers, which appear just before the leaves, are described as white or pink, the white and pink "petals" of dogwood are actually **bracts,** or modified leaves. The true flowers of dogwood are yellow and appear in the center of the showy bracts. In August, they form clusters of glossy red berries; these contrast sharply with the green leaves.

In late summer, dogwood is one of the first trees to show signs of fall color, often blushing on just a few branches. As fall progresses, the whole tree deepens to a vivid crimson. In winter, dogwood is a sculptured form of light gray twigs carrying the clusters of berries until they are eaten by birds. At the ends of the twigs are the flat, gray flower buds that grow larger as spring approaches.

---

**AT A GLANCE**

❖

### FLOWERING DOGWOOD
*Cornus florida*

**Features:** white or pink flowers, red berries

**Foliage:** deciduous

**Outstanding season:** spring

**Height:** 10 to 20 feet

**Spread:** 15 to 20 feet

**Growth rate:** moderate

**Native:** yes

**Range:** Zones 5 to 9

**Light:** partial shade

**Pests:** dogwood borer, anthracnose, sunscald

**Remarks:** an excellent understory tree

*Fall's red foliage, winter's shining berries, and spring's new buds can all be seen on dogwood at one time.*

*Dogwood blossoms seem to float in midair when the tree is in full bloom.*

*The horizontal layers of deep crimson foliage are a hallmark of dogwoods in the fall.*

# In the Landscape

Use dogwood in a naturalistic landscape as you would find it in the wild, setting saplings among existing trees at random, no closer than 15 feet apart. Four or five dogwoods drifted naturally across a lot will create a free-form sweep of bloom and foliage. Dogwoods may also be used as foundation plantings if they are at least 10 to 15 feet from the house and not in direct afternoon sun. They will provide some flowers at eye level to soften architectural lines.

Flowering dogwood is also a good tree to plant around shaded patios or on terraced hillsides. Drift them informally along the length of a driveway and place a splendid specimen in the curve of an entry walkway. Several trees drifted informally will frame a space within an open lawn and naturally create an enclosure with their trunks. While these trees are a good height for use under power lines, they suffer under the full sun that accompanies such locations.

# Dogwood

*Dogwoods come in pink, too.*

## Planting and Care

In the South, dogwoods will not attain their open, layered form if planted in full sun. Instead, they will be more compact and will not grow vigorously. Farther north, where the sun is not so harsh, shade is less critical.

No matter what region of the country you plant in, flowering dogwood needs rich, slightly acid, well-drained soil. Good drainage is a must; plants will die in soggy soils. However, keep the plants watered during drought when you see their leaves drooping.

Dogwoods have very shallow roots, so avoid tilling under the canopy. Instead of trying to grow other plants in the soil around established trees, maintain a 3-inch layer of mulch under the canopy. This will aid moisture retention.

## Different Selections

Among the most popular flowering dogwood selections are Rubra, the first pink dogwood, and Cherokee Chief, which has deep pink bracts. Cherokee Princess is known for its very large white bracts. Cloud Nine is white and blooms profusely even when young. Plena is an unusual white selection that has semidouble bracts. Fragrant Cloud is a white-blooming selection whose flowers are lightly scented. Wonderberry boasts berries about twice the usual size. Welch's Junior Miss is the only pink selection recommended for the lower South.

## Troubleshooting

Avoid hitting the trunk with a mower as open wounds provide access for the dogwood borer, a serious pest that can kill the tree. Turn to page 124 for more about borers.

Anthracnose, a fungal disease, threatens trees in cool, moist climates. In areas where summer temperatures often exceed 90 degrees, the disease is not a problem. The best protection against this disease is to plant cultivars of Kousa dogwood that are resistant.

If at all possible, do not cut down the shade tree that protects a dogwood. This will expose the tree to sunscald damage, since it was accustomed to growing in the shade.

*American dogwood has distinctive, pebblelike bark.*

# Kousa Dogwood

From the Orient comes the demure yet intriguing Kousa dogwood *(Cornus kousa)*, a tree that tends to be slightly smaller—up to 20 feet in height with a smaller spread—than the native flowering dogwood. While it may be smaller, it packs a garden surprise; it blooms as late as May and sometimes June.

## A Closer Look

Kousa dogwood bears white bracts, but unlike the rounded bracts of flowering dogwood, these are pointed and are displayed against the opened leaves. The blooms are carried on stems that may rise 6 inches above the glossy green foliage.

Kousa dogwood has brilliant scarlet fall color, another hallmark of the plant. In late September, a fruit the size of a small cherry develops and hangs at the end of each long stem. Winter brings a better chance to see the bark, which is a deep mahogany. This bark peels back to reveal the light brown inner covering.

## In the Landscape

While it holds landscape interest from a distance, Kousa should be seen up close, beside an entry or in a townhouse courtyard. The way the flowers are displayed makes the tree attractive from above, so consider Kousa as a choice plant to be seen from an elevated deck, an upstairs window, or the lower side of a retaining wall.

The ascending habit of Kousa dogwood makes it useful over a terrace or a patio since the branches will not hang down in your way.

## Planting and Care

Plant Kousa dogwood in the same horticultural conditions of flowering dogwood: partial shade and rich, moist, well-drained soil. In the South, the leaves may curl and turn brown along the edges during the heat of summer.

## Different Selections

Two outstanding selections are Milky Way, a very prolific flowering selection, and Summer Stars, which has bracts that persist for up to six weeks after blooming begins. Aurora, Stellar Pink, and Celestial are three of several hybrids developed from the flowering and Kousa dogwoods. They bloom after flowering dogwood and before Kousa to fill the gap between their seasons. With these hybrids, you can enjoy dogwood blooms for two full months.

*Kousa dogwood, a species that blooms later than flowering dogwood, produces bright red fruit the size of a cherry.*

AT A GLANCE
❖
### KOUSA DOGWOOD
*Cornus kousa*

**Features:** exquisite flowers and fruit
**Foliage:** deciduous
**Outstanding season:** all seasons
**Height:** 20 to 30 feet
**Spread:** 20 to 30 feet
**Growth rate:** slow to medium
**Native:** no
**Range:** Zones 5 to 8
**Light:** partial shade
**Pests:** none specific
**Remarks:** late spring or early summer flowers

# Elm

*The outstanding ornamental bark of Chinese elm gives it the name* lacebark elm.

Chinese elm is a disease-resistant, fast-growing shade tree. Perhaps its most notable asset is its handsome exfoliating bark, which gives it another common name, lacebark elm. As the tree ages, the outer bark flakes off to reveal a patchwork of green, gray, orange, and brown bark underneath.

## A Closer Look

Chinese elm has a somewhat vase-shaped profile when young but becomes more rounded and open as it ages. The tree grows quickly to an average mature height of 40 to 50 feet with a crown spread nearly as great. Young trees may grow as much as 3 feet per year in good conditions.

The tree has small, dark green leaves that give it a fine texture. In fall, the foliage turns a muted yellow or reddish purple, often holding the color into late November and even December along the Gulf Coast. In frost-free parts of Florida and Texas, the tree is evergreen.

## In the Landscape

Because of its tolerance of hot, dry conditions, Chinese elm is an excellent choice for a street planting or for lining a driveway or a long walkway. The spreading vase-shaped branches of the tree allow plenty of clearance beneath. Chinese elm also works well in narrow courtyards where you need shade but have little space. Its ascending branches keep the body of the tree above the typical height of foundations and walls. This makes it a natural choice for decks, terraces, porches, and courtyards. In some locations, this tree is known as "patio elm."

Chinese elm has an extensive shallow root system, making it difficult to maintain a lush lawn beneath the canopy. Mulch the area instead, or plant a competitive ground cover, such as liriope.

## Planting and Care

Chinese elm prefers full sun and tolerates heat, drought, and pollution. While it adapts to many soil types, it grows most rapidly in moist, fertile soil. This tree is tolerant of alkaline soil.

### AT A GLANCE
❖
### CHINESE ELM
*Ulmus parvifolia*

**Features:** graceful branches, beautiful mottled bark

**Foliage:** deciduous

**Outstanding season:** summer, winter

**Height:** 40 to 50 feet, sometimes 70 feet

**Spread:** 30 to 40 feet

**Growth rate:** rapid

**Native:** no

**Range:** Zones 4 to 9

**Light:** full sun

**Pests:** none specific

**Remarks:** tolerates urban conditions

# Different Selections

In the nursery trade, Chinese elm has long been confused with Siberian elm, an inferior, brittle species. Be sure that you take home Chinese elm *(Ulmus parvifolia)* and not Siberian elm *(Ulmus pumila)*. One way to be certain you purchase the right species is to ask for one of the following selections.

Drake has sweeping, nearly pendulous branches and deep green foliage. Sempervirens, also called evergreen Chinese elm, has a rounded crown and a spreading form, while True Green tends to be nearly evergreen and more rounded in habit.

*The vase shape and high branches of Chinese elm make it a perfect tree for shading a terrace.*

# Flowering Peach

*The most popular peach trees are the double-flowered forms.*

The spring brilliance of flowering peach draws the attention of many gardeners, but these trees can be difficult to grow because of their natural susceptibility to diseases and insect pests. Still, this small ornamental peach, a relative of the fruit tree, has an appeal that is not found in other flowering trees. Its dark, gnarled bark and wandering limbs are softened by delicate flowers.

## A Closer Look

The flower color of flowering peach ranges from pink to white, depending on the selection. The blossoms are especially striking against the dark, charcoal-colored bark. The weathered look of the bark gives this tree an artful quality and an interesting look in winter.

Flowering peach has glossy green foliage much like the leaves of its relative, fruiting peach. This is a moderately fast-growing tree that grows 15 to 25 feet high and at least as wide or wider.

---

**AT A GLANCE**
❖
### FLOWERING PEACH
*Prunus persica*

**Features:** spring flowers, dark bark

**Foliage:** deciduous

**Outstanding season:** spring

**Height:** 15 to 25 feet

**Spread:** 20 to 25 feet

**Growth rate:** moderate

**Native:** no

**Range:** Zones 5 to 9

**Light:** full sun

**Pests:** peach tree borer

**Remarks:** a short-lived but showy tree

*The dark bark of flowering peach recedes into the landscape, causing the flowers to appear suspended above the ground.*

## In the Landscape

Use flowering peach as an accent in a garden border where its form will be silhouetted against a wall or a fence, or for seasonal show in the lawn or near a patio. However, flowering peach does not live very long, often lasting only 10 years before succumbing to insects or diseases. Consider it a temporary planting and do not plant it as the focus of a garden where its loss would leave a gaping hole.

## Planting and Care

Flowering peach prefers full sun. To be sure that the tree lives as long as possible, plant it in well-drained, fertile soil; it will not grow in soggy locations. However, it is tolerant of various soil types—sandy or clay—provided it is well drained.

## Different Selections

There are several selections of flowering peach available for the home landscape. They include Alba, which has white, single flowers and Alboplena, which has white double flowers. There are numerous other forms, some weeping, some bicolored, and some with double red or pink flowers.

## Troubleshooting

Flowering peach is susceptible to peach tree borers. See page 124 for more information about borers.

*Flowering peach puts on a brilliant show in early spring alongside pansies.*

# Fringe Tree

*The panicles of fringe tree look like beards.*

Fringe tree will take you by surprise. This small, sometimes shrubby tree wears an unusual fleecy dangle of fragrant white blooms that are nearly as finely cut as Spanish moss. It is a tree you never forget after you see—and smell—its blooms.

## A Closer Look

The long, white panicles of this tree look like small "beards." Other names for this tree include Grancy gray beard, old man's beard, and granddaddy's gray beard.

The delicate flowers appear in midspring. Male trees have larger, showier beards than female trees but lack the clusters of blue, olivelike fruit that hang behind the foliage in late summer.

The leaves are medium green on top and slightly lighter on the underside, up to 8 inches long, and tapered. In the wild, the large leaves and the tendency of the plant to colonize are a key to identification. In fall, the foliage turns yellow and has a slightly luminescent quality.

## In the Landscape

Fringe tree is an unanticipated accent in a shrub border. Because it grows to a maximum height of only 12 to 20 feet, it can be effective in tree form or as a multitrunked shrubby plant. It is particularly effective in wooded, natural planting schemes. Simply set it among existing trees to be a counterpoint to larger spring blooms or an evergreen background.

Plant it with rhododendrons or azaleas—it prefers the same cultural conditions—and its casual habit and profuse blooms will be shown off nicely by the foliage of these popular shrubs. You may also bring it into the open as a feature tree in a perennial border.

## Planting and Care

Plant fringe tree in rich, well-drained, slightly acid soil. It will also tolerate damp soil; in the wild, it is often found along stream banks. Although an understory plant in the wild, fringe tree will also grow in full sun.

New plants do not bloom until they are three to five years old. The tree is also one of the last to sprout leaves in the spring.

---

AT A GLANCE

❖

### FRINGE TREE
*Chionanthus virginicus*

**Features:** fleecy, fragrant flowers
**Foliage:** deciduous
**Outstanding season:** spring
**Height:** 12 to 20 feet
**Spread:** 12 to 20 feet
**Growth rate:** slow
**Native:** yes
**Range:** Zones 3 to 9
**Light:** full sun to partial shade
**Pests:** none specific
**Remarks:** tolerates wet soil

*The rounded crown of fringe tree is covered with fleecy white flowers in midspring.*

## Species and Selections

Fringe tree is generally available only as the species; there are very few named selections. Chinese fringe tree *(Chionanthus retusus)* is a different species that is hardy to Zone 5. The blooms are upright clusters of flowers. It grows slightly larger than fringe tree and may be grown as a small tree, although it is typically a shrub. The leaves are slightly smaller than those of fringe tree.

# Ginkgo

*The fan-shaped leaves of ginkgo are the tree's identifying feature.*

Ginkgo is a living curiosity whose leaves have been found in fossils dating back 150 million years. Today it is treasured by gardeners for its glorious fall color, unusual form, and uniquely shaped leaves. A rugged tree capable of withstanding urban conditions, ginkgo (also called maidenhair tree) is popular as a street planting or for use in parks but it is certainly not limited to those locations. If you have the patience to let it outgrow the sparse, helter-skelter branching structure of its youth, the tree will grow to a long-lived, large, and full shade tree.

## A Closer Look

Autumn is ginkgo's most spectacular season, when it wears a mantle of golden yellow leaves. The tree's vivid show is due in part to the even coloration of the leaves, with rare variation in hue. These may all drop within a day, carpeting the ground beneath the tree in a circle of gold.

However, it need not be fall for you to notice ginkgo. Its unusual form is equally eye-catching, as its branches grow with unpredictable angles following no discernible pattern. The tree is sparsely limbed, without a network of fine twigs, and the relatively open crown allows the wayward branching to remain visible. As the tree grows older, it fills out to form a more dense crown and grows anywhere from 50 to 70 feet tall and 30 to 40 feet wide.

The leaves closely adhere to stout stems and major branches in clusters of three to five. They emerge bright green in early spring, opening into the characteristic 2- to 3½-inch-long fan shape that is divided into two distinct lobes. The foliage remains bright green on both sides of the leaf until fall.

## In the Landscape

This is an ideal tree for large properties or gardens where a corner may be set aside to allow a tree to fully develop. Ginkgos are also well placed on country lots with long driveways, where they serve as landscape features along the way to the house.

Plant ginkgo in a prominent space in the open lawn. The tree's erratic branching is beautiful from below; plant the tree on the crown of a hill or at the top of a drive, where the branches will be silhouetted against the sky. Take advantage of its glorious fall color by planting it where the foliage can be seen against a dark background, such as deep pine woods or dark brick.

## AT A GLANCE

### GINKGO
*Ginkgo biloba*

**Features:** angular branching, disease free, rich fall color

**Foliage:** deciduous

**Outstanding season:** fall

**Height:** 50 to 80 feet

**Spread:** at least 30 feet

**Growth rate:** slow to moderate

**Native:** no

**Range:** Zones 3 to 9

**Light:** full sun

**Pests:** none specific

**Remarks:** tolerates urban conditions

## Planting and Care

Perhaps one reason this ancient tree has survived is that it can adapt to harsh conditions. Although it will grow fastest in rich, moist soil, it will adapt to poor sandy or heavy clay soil, either alkaline or acid. You may encourage faster growth with regular watering and fertilizer in the spring.

## Troubleshooting

Ginkgo is *dioecious,* meaning male and female flowers are borne on different trees. The only drawback to ginkgo is that the fruit of female trees smells like rotten eggs. Sometimes this fruit does not appear for the first 20 years, but eventually it will if you have a female tree. The only way to avoid this is to plant a male tree.

## Different Selections

Autumn Gold is a broad, spreading male tree with splendid fall color. Lakeview is a compact, conical male; Sentry is an upright male tree.

*A young ginkgo is oddly interesting, with limbs growing at irregular angles. Later the tree fills out to form a fuller canopy.*

# Hawthorn

*The berries of Washington hawthorn hang in lovely clusters along the branches.*

Hawthorns tuck themselves away and wait until winter to make garden headlines. Actually a large group of species and hybrids, two species of the large hawthorn family are particularly suited to the home landscape, Washington hawthorn (*Crataegus phaenopyrum*) and a cultivar of green hawthorn named Winter King (*Crataegus viridis* Winter King).

The hallmark of these small native trees is not their flowers, which do produce a handsome show, but their abundant, bright red berries. These appear on the tree in August but are most visible in autumn, after the leaves have fallen. Suspended against the winter sky, these bright scarlet ornaments are quite beautiful. The berries will last through the winter if you keep your bird feeder filled to distract the birds.

## A Closer Look

Both of these trees are thorny and twiggy. The flowers are white and appear in clusters along the branches and at the end of each branch. Both trees have handsome, deep green foliage and cast a light shade that permits grasses to grow beneath them. In fall, both Washington and Winter King hawthorn turn a range of colors, ending in purple and scarlet.

Winter King hawthorn is an "improved" version of the native green hawthorn that looks much like Washington hawthorn. It is a more vase-shaped selection, though it reaches about the same size (20 to 25 feet). The flowers are borne in 2-inch clusters along the branches in late spring. Winter King produces fruits that are slightly larger than those of Washington hawthorn. These berries are red when mature, eventually becoming orange red in winter. One very noticeable difference between these two hawthorns is that the bark of Winter King, a lovely silvery gray, flakes off to reveal an orange-brown color beneath.

Washington hawthorn does best in full sun or partial shade. The foliage opens a soft reddish purple before turning to a deep, lustrous green. The flowers follow, appearing from late May to

*The flowers of Washington hawthorn open after the deep green foliage appears.*

| AT A GLANCE |
| :---: |
| ❖ |
| **HAWTHORN** |
| *Crataegus species* |

**Features:** handsome flowers, fruit, and bark

**Foliage:** deciduous

**Outstanding season:** spring, fall, winter

**Height:** 25 to 30 feet

**Spread:** 20 to 25 feet

**Growth rate:** moderate

**Native:** yes

**Range:** Zones 4 to 9

**Light:** full to partial shade

**Pests:** orange rust

**Remarks:** beautiful winter show of berries

mid-June. This is the last hawthorn to bloom, and the clusters of small white flowers appear like cotton balls amid the deep green background.

In fall, the foliage is a spectacular, vivid scarlet; in the South, the leaves take on more of a purple hue. The fruits are about ¼ inch in diameter and are suspended in clusters along the branches.

## In the Landscape

Hawthorns offer year-round interest. They are excellent, if slightly unusual, specimen trees because they are so thorny. Both Washington and Winter King hawthorn will bring splendid returns when planted in a border that shelters a bird bath or at the lawn's edge, poised before a dark background. Set a hawthorn in the corner of a wooden

*Hawthorns are good choices for narrow courtyards where their abundant fruit can be seen up close.*

*The exfoliating bark of Winter King hawthorn has an outstanding effect in a small space.*

fence, with the tree's beautiful bark and profuse berries set off against the weathered wood. Keep the background in mind for these trees; silhouette them against the side of the house, against a tall wall, or along a fence. A dark background will make the fruit appear even more vivid.

Plant hawthorns at least 10 to 12 feet away from a structure. Because of their thorns, avoid placing hawthorns in high-traffic areas or prune the low branches. One of the best locations for a hawthorn is just outside a window. Cedar waxwings, grosbeaks, cardinals, and mockingbirds will line up to dine on the fruit. It is unusual to see a hawthorn without a bird nest tucked away in the tangle of thorny upper branches.

Use several hawthorns in a group as a feature in an open lawn, a formation that is particularly attractive if the winter backdrop of the plants shows off the color of the berries. They also serve admirably as a tall screen to block an undesirable view. The plants respond very well to pruning—a trait that allows them to be espaliered on a wall or a fence.

## Planting and Care

Given full sun and well-drained soil, hawthorn is easy to grow. Although it prefers moist, fertile soil, it will tolerate dry, poor soil and urban pollution; this makes hawthorn a good choice for street-side plantings.

## Other Species

Parsley hawthorn *(Crataegus marshallii)* is usually a multi-trunked small tree with white flowers. It has beautiful exfoliating bark, like that of crape myrtle, and the foliage looks like parsley. This tree is better suited to the warm, humid climate of the lower South than most other hawthorns.

## Troubleshooting

Hawthorn is a host of orange rust, a disease that needs the cohost of red cedar. The infestation causes orange bristles to form on the hawthorn's fruit and twigs, which then turn brown and die. The best solution is to remove all red cedar *(Juniperus virginiana)* within several hundred yards of the hawthorn, or spray the hawthorns according to the recommendations of your local Extension agent.

# Hemlock

*The small needles and fine branches
of hemlock lend it to pruning.*

Canadian hemlock is one of the only needle-leafed evergreen trees that retains its foliage and full form in shady locations. Fortunately, this large native tree adapts to locations beyond its cool mountain habitat; it is a suitable evergreen for screening throughout the country.

## A Closer Look

The needles of Canadian hemlock, which are less than 1 inch long, lie flat along the stems. The needles are lime green when they emerge in early spring, changing quickly to dark glossy green. They give the tree a dark but finely textured look.

As hemlocks age, they gradually lose their lower limbs to reveal the deeply furrowed and ridged bark that is characteristic of mature trees. Expect the tree to grow from 40 to 70 feet tall, spreading at its base to nearly 35 feet. The tree may soar more than 25 feet in height in as little as 15 years. If unpruned, the branches will drape gracefully all the way to the ground.

## In the Landscape

Where you live determines how you use hemlock in the landscape. In the Piedmont, which is about as far south as Canadian hemlock can grow reliably, it must be shaded during the heat of the day. In the mountains of the upper South and Mid-Atlantic, Canadian hemlock will grow in sunnier locations.

Canadian hemlock also fills an important design niche in the colder portions of the Piedmont—that of a tall evergreen understory tree. Plant it to create an evergreen backdrop for spring-flowering plants, such as dogwood, or the deep brown leaves of beech in the winter.

You may also plant Canadian hemlock as a screen for privacy. However, do not plant hemlock closer than 20 feet to the house or you will need to trim branches from the base and thus diminish its pyramidal form. The tree is too large to grow near power lines.

Where Canadian hemlock will grow in full sun, you may use it as a windbreak or an evergreen screen. In fact, it is possible to maintain a planting of hemlock trees as a sheared, formal hedge. Although this requires regular trimming, it is a sure way to have a high wall of green in a formal garden.

### AT A GLANCE
❖
### CANADIAN HEMLOCK
*Tsuga canadensis*

**Features:** pyramidal form, needlelike leaves

**Foliage:** evergreen

**Outstanding season:** all seasons

**Height:** 40 to 70 feet

**Spread:** 25 to 35 feet

**Growth rate:** medium

**Native:** yes

**Range:** Zones 3 to 7

**Light:** full sun in the North, shade in the South

**Pests:** spider mites, scales, bagworms

**Remarks:** makes a graceful screen

*Hemlock serves well as a finely textured evergreen background and screen.*

Plant these trees along the driveway of a large property. Their constant green is a dependable backdrop to a bird feeder or a border of flowers and shrubs and will nicely frame garden statuary.

## Planting and Care

Plant Canadian hemlock in moist, well-drained, acid soil that is rich in organic matter. In full sun, the tree must be sheltered from drying wind. If your soil is heavy, leave the top half of the hemlock rootball above ground level and mound the soil around it. Then mulch with a 2- to 3-inch layer of bark or pine straw and water regularly. Adequate moisture is the key to hemlock's survival, as young trees are very susceptible to drought.

The first two years are critical to the tree's growth. It is a good idea to have a nursery install and guarantee balled-and-burlapped plants rather than planting them yourself. Canadian hemlock will survive as far south as Zone 7 if provided shade and regular waterings during hot, dry weather.

Canadian hemlock is sometimes available as a live Christmas tree. If you want to transplant it successfully after the holiday, keep the time indoors to only a week and shear one-third to one-half of the foliage before planting.

## Species and Selections

Sargent's weeping hemlock (*Tsuga canadensis* Pendula) is a slow-growing mounding plant with extremely graceful branches. Carolina hemlock *(Tsuga caroliniana)* is a slightly smaller species with a softer texture and more pyramidal form. Carolina hemlock is more sensitive to heat than Canadian hemlock.

## Troubleshooting

Hemlocks may be bothered by spider mites, scales, and bagworms. See pages 124 and 125 for more about these pests. Be sure to water trees during drought, especially in the southern limits of their range.

# Holly

The spiny leaves and red berries of holly have become a symbol of Christmas, a high compliment to the evergreen members of this genus during the leafless months. Many evergreen hollies have the familiar pyramidal form and glossy green foliage with a varying number of spines along the edges of the leaves. These trees are also noted for their smooth, gray bark. Deciduous hollies are more sparsely foliated and their leaves are rounded, spineless, and lighter green.

Most hollies are dioecious; the male and female flowers appear on separate plants. The female flower produces the berries, but only if pollinated by a suitable male flower. To guarantee berries, there must be a male holly of the same species within 30 to 40 yards of the female tree. Pollen-laden bees will cover the distance between them.

## American Holly

This native evergreen is a reliable landscape tree, although there are many newer selections that have a more profuse show of berries. American holly slowly grows to at least 25 feet but may ultimately tower at 50 feet. It has green, spiny leaves and light gray bark. In full sun, the plant is dense; in shade it is much more open in habit. The layered look of the foliage is a subtle feature that has yet to be repeated in the newer selections.

## In the Landscape

American holly and its selections make an excellent feature plant either singly or in a group. It is particularly effective as a freestanding lawn specimen. Do not prune; let the branches drape to the ground to achieve the tree's full, graceful form. Because of its wide base a tree used in this manner needs an expanse of open lawn.

American holly dresses up the landscape and provides a visual anchor during winter. The plant works well to frame a winter vista from indoors by directing your eye to the bright sparkle of the fruit and the steady gloss of the foliage. Plant the tree in your line of sight along a garden walk or a long driveway.

## Planting and Care

American holly prefers slightly acid, well-drained soil that is rich in organic matter and remains moist. It will also tolerate poor, sandy soil but will not thrive in heavy soil that traps water against the roots. American holly will grow in full sun or partial shade but should not be planted in windy, dry locations where the foliage may dry out.

*American holly is a towering tree.*

### AT A GLANCE
### AMERICAN HOLLY
*Ilex opaca*

**Features:** vivid foliage and fruit
**Foliage:** evergreen
**Outstanding season:** winter
**Height:** 40 to 50 feet
**Spread:** 18 to 40 feet
**Growth rate:** medium
**Native:** yes
**Range:** Zones 5 to 9
**Light:** full sun to partial shade
**Pests:** none specific
**Remarks:** stately, pyramidal

*Hybrid Foster holly is better suited to small properties than the native American holly, its parent.*

## AT A GLANCE

❖

### FOSTER HOLLY
*Ilex* x *attenuata* Foster #2

**Features:** narrow, dark green leaves; profuse berries

**Foliage:** evergreen

**Outstanding season:** winter

**Height:** 25 to 40 feet

**Spread:** 10 to 15 feet

**Growth rate:** rapid

**Native:** a hybrid of native hollies

**Range:** Zones 6 to 9

**Light:** full sun to partial shade

**Pests:** none specific

**Remarks:** good for screening

# Different Selections

Croonenburg is a compact, columnar tree that is *monoecious;* both male and female flowers are borne on the same plant. It bears fruit heavily every year. Greenleaf is known for its handsome glossy foliage and bright berries.

# Foster Holly

Foster holly is a hybrid between American holly and Dahoon holly (*Ilex cassine*) that is shorter and more narrow than American holly; often the tree will have a double trunk that grows rapidly to 25 feet high. The tree has narrow, lance-shaped leaves that are deep green with a slightly blue cast. The leaves are less spiny along the margins than those of American holly and are glossy on the top side. The smaller size and neat foliage add to the popularity of this tree.

There are actually several Foster hybrids. Foster #2 and Foster #3 are female plants that can produce a very heavy berry crop and are usually the trees you will find labeled simply as Foster. (Foster #4 is a male plant which, if planted nearby, helps berry production.) The bluish cast to the foliage enhances the berry show, which can last through winter. However, it is Foster #2 that is most readily available at nurseries and garden centers.

# In the Landscape

The narrow habit of young Foster holly may lead you to think that it will work in foundation plantings as close as 4 feet to the building. This is too close, as Foster holly grows quickly. The close siting will cause the tree to lean precipitously away from the house. Plant it at least 8 feet from the house.

This narrow tree works well on small lots, providing evergreen screening between adjoining properties without encroaching on the limited space. It also can be worked into a border without over-whelming the garden's edge as the plant ages, during which time the branching becomes less pyramidal and the tree has a more loose, relaxed form. As it matures, Foster holly can be a good open-lawn specimen on a small lot.

# Planting and Care

Plant Foster holly in moist but well-drained acid soil that is rich in organic matter. This tree does well in full sun and remains fuller than other hollies in partially shaded locations.

# Savannah Holly

The Savannah holly is a half sister of Foster holly, but you would never guess it to look at this broader leafed, much lighter green tree. It has a looser, more relaxed look than Foster holly, and is not as stately and reserved as American holly.

Savannah holly grows rapidly to 25 to 30 feet tall. Its base is wider than that of Foster holly but not as wide as that of American holly. In form it is pyramidal and its foliage is loosely layered. Like Foster holly, Savannah holly produces berries profusely.

## In the Landscape

Plant Savannah holly where you would use American holly but have less space. Place it where several paths converge, or use it to soften masonry walls. This is a good plant for the open lawn, but it will not bring the dignity that American holly brings to open grounds. Savannah holly works as a centerpiece in formal gardens where you want to maintain formality, yet seek a look that is slightly more relaxed than that of American holly.

## Planting and Care

Savannah holly prefers full sun but will grow in partial shade. It is quite tolerant of heat and high humidity and is well adapted to the lower and coastal South. Give this tree moist but well-drained, slightly acid soil and it will thrive.

Savannah holly does not like to be moved and will drop leaves if transplanted. This does not mean that it is dead; be patient and continue watering.

## Related Hybrids

East Palatka is a naturally occurring hybrid with similar parentage to Foster holly. Discovered near Palatka, Florida, this is a female plant featuring broad, flat, dark green leaves with few spines. It is a good selection for hot climates. Hume holly has rounded, almost spineless leaves and small red berries. It is pyramidal and informal, growing rapidly to a mature height of nearly 30 feet.

*Savannah holly is loosely pyramidal in form.*

*Savannah holly bears profuse berries. The foliage is a lighter green than that of Foster holly or American holly.*

### AT A GLANCE
#### ❖
### SAVANNAH HOLLY
*Ilex x attenuata* Savannah

**Features:** fast growing, produces many berries

**Foliage:** evergreen

**Outstanding season:** winter

**Height:** 25 to 30 feet

**Spread:** 10 to 15 feet

**Growth rate:** rapid

**Native:** a hybrid of native hollies

**Range:** Zones 6 to 9

**Light:** full sun to partial shade

**Pests:** none specific

**Remarks:** good for smaller properties

*Possum haw's vivid berries are borne in clusters along the tree's gray stems.*

# Possum Haw

Possum haw is a surprising holly—it does not have spiny, evergreen leaves. It is a twiggy, deciduous holly whose show is not dependent upon its leaves; possum haw is grown for its berries.

Native to Southern wetlands and swamps, this often multi-trunked small tree will grow rapidly to 15 feet tall and nearly as broad. Possum haw may grow as much as 10 feet taller in the wild. The growth habit is always the same: an upright, arching form with a broader crown and smaller trunks than crape myrtle.

The foliage is dark glossy green in summer, turning yellow in fall. The tree is inconspicuous until September, when its ⅓-inch-diameter fruits begin to ripen on female plants. By the time the leaves drop, the fruits are a splendidly vivid orange to deep red. In winter, possum haw seems to glow red. The berries persist on the bare gray stems through the winter or until eaten by birds.

## In the Landscape

This plant perks up the winter border, particularly in front of a dark evergreen backdrop, such as Leyland cypress or red cedar, or the weathered siding of an outbuilding. Use possum haw against a wall, such as the side of a garage, before the backdrop of darkened winter woods, or in front of a split-rail fence.

Possum haw naturalizes extremely well, so mix it into drifts of existing trees. Since it lacks year-round interest, use possum haw as a supplemental planting, not a feature tree.

---

### AT A GLANCE
❖
### POSSUM HAW
*Ilex decidua*

**Features:** brilliant berries
**Foliage:** deciduous
**Outstanding season:** winter
**Height:** 15 to 25 feet
**Spread:** 8 to 20 feet
**Growth rate:** rapid
**Native:** yes
**Range:** Zones 4 to 9
**Light:** full sun
**Pests:** none specific
**Remarks:** good for wet soils

*Possum haw is an oversized outdoor arrangement of berries in winter.*

78

## Planting and Care

Possum haw needs full sun to produce the most berries, but it will grow in partial shade. Unlike other hollies, which prefer acid soil, possum haw will tolerate alkaline soil. Because it is a swamp plant it is useful in wet sites, but it will also perform well in any normal garden soil. Only the female plant has berries. Plant a male tree nearby to ensure berry production.

## Different Selections

Warren's Red has very dark green foliage and bright red berries. Council Fire is an outstanding selection with long-lasting fruit.

# Winterberry

Winterberry has the same shrubby form as star magnolia. Like possum haw, winterberry is deciduous but has stiffer stems. It is upright, creating a broadly arching crown of wide, deep green leaves. It grows to about 10 feet tall by 10 feet wide with many suckers from the base that form large, multistemmed trunks.

The foliage is medium green and has little color in the fall. It turns black after the first frost and is often called black alder. Female trees have bright red, 1/4-inch berries that are held along the stems in pairs during the winter.

## In the Landscape

Use winterberry as you would possum haw to perk up the winter border, particularly in front of a dark evergreen backdrop or against a wall.

If you have a rock wall, plant winterberry nearby either singly or in a group. The tree also works well beside a creek or a pond.

## Planting and Care

Winterberry will grow in wet areas with moist, slightly acid soil that is rich in organic matter. It is indifferent to heavy or light soil and will grow in full sun or partial shade. Be sure to provide a male plant for good berry production.

## Different Selections

Afterglow is a compact tree with orange-red fruit. Harvest Red is a red-fruited hybrid with deep red-purple fall color. Sparkleberry forms a multistemmed shrub with abundant fruit. Winter Red is known for bright yellow fall color and large, long-lasting berries.

*The berries of winterberry are often held in pairs, which distinguishes this holly from possum haw.*

AT A GLANCE

❖

## WINTERBERRY
*Ilex verticillata*

**Features:** brilliant berries
**Foliage:** deciduous
**Outstanding season:** winter
**Height:** 6 to 10 feet
**Spread:** 6 to 10 feet
**Growth rate:** moderate
**Native:** yes
**Range:** Zones 3 to 9
**Light:** full sun to partial shade
**Pests:** none specific
**Remarks:** good for wet soils

# Leyland Cypress

*Leyland cypress works well as a trimmed hedge.*

No tree makes a faster evergreen screen than Leyland cypress. It grows rapidly while maintaining a narrow pyramidal form and dense, dark green foliage. It also thrives in many different soil conditions—sandy to heavy clay, acid to alkaline—as long as the soil is well drained.

## A Closer Look

The only thing that changes about this steady, rocket-shaped evergreen is its size. A tree may grow as much as 3 feet in a season. Poor soil slows its growth slightly, but in rich soil with adequate moisture the tree can shoot past 30 feet in about 10 years.

The new spring growth of Leyland cypress has a lighter hue than the mature dark green foliage. The leaves are flattened along the stems and are very tiny; the branches are angled slightly upward from the central **leader,** or primary shoot from the trunk. Unlike many evergreens with scaly leaves, the foliage of Leyland cypress is not prickly.

From a distance, the form of Leyland cypress calls to mind a young red cedar. But Leyland cypress holds its shape at maturity, while older red cedars lose their compact form.

## In the Landscape

Leyland cypress is the consummate evergreen hedge tree. Several trees planted at 10-foot intervals will grow together to screen any objectionable view beyond the line of the planting. Planted in this fashion, it also becomes an evergreen backdrop for smaller trees, flowering shrubs, and flower beds. Because it is much taller than it is wide, you may use it along a property line to provide privacy from neighboring two-story houses.

Use Leyland cypress as the formal "living columns" to a driveway or to soften the corners of a house (plant it at least 10 feet from the house). It also makes an interesting vertical accent when contrasted with broad, spreading trees, such as Yoshino cherry.

---

### AT A GLANCE
❖
### LEYLAND CYPRESS
#### x *Cupressocyparis leylandii*

**Features:** rapid growth; narrow, upright form

**Foliage:** evergreen

**Outstanding season:** all seasons

**Height:** 50 to 60 feet, may reach more than 100 feet

**Spread:** 10 to 15 feet

**Growth rate:** rapid

**Native:** no

**Range:** Zones 6 to 10

**Light:** full sun

**Pests:** bagworms, canker

**Remarks:** a very fast-growing screen

## Planting and Care

Plant Leyland cypress in any well-drained soil. It will grow quickly when there is plenty of water available, but it will rot in poorly drained soil. Although hardy in the middle South, temperatures of 20 degrees below zero or lower will damage the tree.

## Different Selections

Naylor's Blue is a selection with a handsome bluish cast to the foliage. Naylor's Weeping has a pendulous form.

## Troubleshooting

If you live in an area where ice storms are frequent, select plants with a single main trunk. Multitrunked plants will bend and may even split in icy conditions. When this happens, you can tie the trunks together to hold them erect again.

Bagworms, small caterpillars living inside a twiggy bag that hangs on the stems, will chew the foliage of Leyland cypress. Turn to caterpillars, pages 124–125, for more information about bagworms. If you notice that the branches are mysteriously dying, your tree may be infected with Ceridium canker, a disease that will eventually kill the tree. Branches begin to die randomly and you may see sap oozing from the trunk. The only solution is to replace the tree.

*Leyland cypress is small enough for a container for about one season; then you must plant it in the ground.*

# Linden

*Littleleaf linden is a shower of gold in fall.*

One of the stalwart trees of European cities, littleleaf linden is also a popular choice for street plantings in America. This tree grows up to 60 feet tall and is tolerant of the disturbed soil and often polluted conditions of city planting sites. Its predictable growth habit makes littleleaf linden a good choice for any city neighborhood, as well as for harsh suburban and rural locations.

## A Closer Look

Littleleaf linden is a dependable shade tree for the middle and upper South. While its slightly fragrant flowers are somewhat noteworthy because they hang from the branches in pendulous clusters, they are not particularly ostentatious. However, the peculiar elongated bracts that descend from the tree will catch your eye because they make the tree look as though it has two entirely different leaves.

The true leaves are heart shaped with toothed edges. They are 3 inches long and usually as broad. The color of the leaves is a shiny dark green that turns yellowish green to gold in the fall.

It is the steady, consistent form of littleleaf linden that earns it high marks in the landscape. Young trees have a marked pyramidal shape that eventually becomes a more upright, rounded form as the years progress. The tree typically branches from a climbable height and reaches upward and outward, casting a medium to deep shade.

In winter, the tree is a study of fine branches and deeply ridged gray-brown bark.

## In the Landscape

Littleleaf linden's neat and orderly appearance lends it to uses where the form is repeated, such as a street planting or along driveways. In a garden with a symmetrical pattern, littleleaf linden will emphasize the formal theme by its consistently oval form.

Plant single trees as specimens in the lawn or where the driveway joins the street. Older houses in city neighborhoods where lawn space is tight may be enhanced by a planting of littleleaf linden.

## Planting and Care

Littleleaf linden prefers moist, well-drained, fertile soil and full sun. It tolerates both alkaline and acid soils. Because it is unaffected by air pollution or compacted ground, it is well suited for city sites. If you plant more than one, allow at least 35 feet between the trees.

## Different Selections

Chancellor is a fast-growing selection with a narrow crown when young. Glenleven also grows rapidly and is known for its very straight trunk. Greenspire is probably the most common selection, popular for its slightly smaller size.

American linden *(Tilia americana),* also known as basswood, is native to Eastern and Midwestern forests. This is a large tree that reaches 60 to 80 feet tall with a 40-foot spread and forms a boxy, upright crown. Although native, American linden is inferior to little-leaf linden as a landscape tree. Its leaves turn brown and drop in late summer, creating a litter problem, and the tree is not as tolerant of city conditions.

*As a street tree, littleleaf linden brings a remarkable uniformity to the landscape.*

# Magnolia

*Southern magnolia seedpods split open as the bright red seeds swell into maturity, usually in October or November.*

When you think of magnolias, you probably envision the stately Southern magnolia with its fragrant, late-spring blooms. But this group of useful landscape plants also includes medium-sized evergreens that are ideal for shading patios, large-leafed deciduous trees, and profusely flowering Oriental hybrids. In short, there is a magnolia for every garden.

## A Closer Look

Magnolias can be divided into several groups, determined by shared traits and uses. The first group is the evergreen native magnolias, which include the massive Southern magnolia, a very large tree, and the more versatile sweetbay magnolia, a multitrunked smaller leafed tree. Evergreen natives bear fragrant blooms in late spring or early summer. Use them as feature trees in the open lawn or as evergreen screens.

The second group is the deciduous native magnolias. Among these are bigleaf magnolia, sporting leaves nearly three feet long and a foot wide, and cucumber tree, a surprising and underappreciated magnolia that makes a fine shade tree.

Choose from the third group, deciduous Oriental magnolias, if you want spring flowers as an accent in a garden border or as an early sign of spring. This group includes star magnolia, saucer magnolia, and lily magnolia. These showy imports are predominantly multitrunked and bloom early in the season, before the foliage emerges.

Except for lily magnolia, which blooms late in the season, Oriental magnolias are so eager to bloom that cold snaps often kill the flowers. You may avoid this by planting them in the coolest area of your yard that receives summer sun, usually on the north or northeast side of the residence. This will reduce the likelihood that warm afternoon sun will coax the plant into bloom before temperatures are warm enough to sustain it. Avoid planting the tree near walls or paving or other surfaces that might radiate warmth. Do not plant the tree in low spots where frost tends to form.

There are also many hybrid magnolias that do not fall into a particular group, as they are crosses between species.

In spite of their differences, all magnolias prefer slightly acid soil that is rich in organic matter. They are also remarkably free of any diseases and insect pests and will thrive in either full sun or partial shade.

# Southern Magnolia

Southern magnolia, a Southern native, is the region's signature evergreen. A large, distinctive tree, it grows into a monumental pyramid of glossy foliage. In late spring or early summer, waxy white blooms cover the tree and release their distinctive, lemony-sweet fragrance. The flowers are large (6 to 10 inches across) and are followed by upright, conelike seedpods with bright red berries inside.

The leaves are 5 to 8 inches long, widened in the middle, with glossy, dark green color, leathery texture and fuzzy, dark brown undersides. Gardeners value the foliage for evergreen cuttings for arrangements.

## In the Landscape

Because of its coarse texture and large size, Southern magnolia is effective both from a distance and up close. For most gardens, a single Southern magnolia planted as an evergreen accent at the edge of the garden or as a specimen in the open lawn is enough. Give it plenty of room; plant it at least 30 feet from the house.

Southern magnolias will fill distant corners or block unsightly views. If your house is at the top of a hill, plant a Southern magnolia at the bottom. A large house at the end of a long driveway will be off-set nicely by magnolias flanked at either side, which lend a stately, dignified character to the home.

Southern magnolia is also a good tree for a beach planting, as it is actually native to the dunes along the East Coast. Its dense foliage will block wind and salt spray year-round, especially when planted in groups of five or more. However, do not rely on Southern magnolia for quick screening; the plant grows very slowly. Also, do not plant it near a patio, as it drops leaves and debris.

## Planting and Care

Southern magnolia prefers well-drained soil that is rich in organic matter. Protect it from winter winds from Nashville northward.

It is better not to remove the lower limbs of a Southern magnolia in order to plant beneath it; let the limbs grow close to the ground to hide the continual drop of leaves and seedpods. The dense surface roots and deep shade make growing anything under the tree nearly impossible.

*The waxy flowers of Southern magnolia have a glorious fragrance.*

### AT A GLANCE

#### SOUTHERN MAGNOLIA
*Magnolia grandiflora*

**Features:** dark leaves, fragrant flowers

**Foliage:** evergreen

**Outstanding season:** summer

**Height:** 20 to 80 feet

**Spread:** 12 to 50 feet

**Growth rate:** slow to moderate

**Native:** yes

**Range:** Zones 6 to 10

**Light:** full sun to partial shade

**Pests:** none specific

**Remarks:** subject to winter burn

*The white flowers of sweetbay magnolia perfume the entire garden.*

AT A GLANCE
❖
## SWEETBAY MAGNOLIA
*Magnolia virginiana*

**Features:** dark green foliage with white undersides, white flowers

**Foliage:** deciduous, evergreen in southern part of range

**Outstanding season:** summer

**Height:** 20 to 60 feet, tallest in southern part of range

**Spread:** 15 to 20 feet

**Growth rate:** moderate

**Native:** yes

**Range:** Zones 5 to 9

**Light:** full sun

**Pests:** none specific

**Remarks:** blooms have a lemony scent

## Different Selections

Edith Bogue is the most cold-hardy selection of Southern magnolia. Braken's Brown Beauty is also cold hardy and is popular for its fuzzy leaf undersides. It has small leaves and grows to about 40 feet tall. Glen St. Mary has attractive leaves with bronze undersides and blooms earlier in its life cycle than most Southern magnolias. Little Gem has small leaves and grows to a height of about 40 feet.

Husse has an upright habit and works well in narrow spaces. Majestic Beauty blooms profusely, and Samuel Sommer has 14-inch flowers. Other selections include Claudia Wannamaker and Gloriosa.

# Sweetbay Magnolia

Sweetbay magnolia is easily indentified by the shimmer of the silvery undersides of its dark green leaves. Evergreen in the coastal and lower South, sweetbay magnolia loses its leaves from the middle South northward. This native is prized for its foliage, its form, and its smooth silver-gray bark. Its lemony-sweet blooms last from late spring into summer and perfume the garden. The spent blooms become handsome seed pods festooned with bright red seeds.

## In the Landscape

Although it may grow to 60 feet tall in the wild, sweetbay magnolia will generally stay much smaller in a garden setting, only 10 to 30 feet tall. Use this tree as an accent planting or a small shade tree for either patios or courtyards. Such close settings take advantage of the fragrance of the creamy white blossoms. The multitrunked form is especially effective for screen plantings, particularly in the southern portion of its range, where it is consistently evergreen.

## Planting and Care

The native habitat of sweetbay magnolia is the highly organic, moist soil of coastal plain swamps, and it prefers the same conditions in the garden. This plant also likes full sun but will do very well in partial shade. In Tennessee and Kentucky and locations farther north, it should be protected from freezing winter winds.

## Different Selections

Recommended selections include Havener, which produces double flowers, and Opelousas, whose flowers and leaves are quite large. Henry Hicks is evergreen to Zone 5.

# Bigleaf Magnolia

Bigleaf magnolia is one of the most aptly named and curiously attractive trees around. Its hallmark, huge, deciduous leaves, can be 1 to 3 feet long and a foot wide, giving it an exotic appearance even in its native woods. In a garden it is quite a conversation piece.

Although this tree is grown more for its foliage than its flowers, the ivory-colored, goblet-shaped blooms are quite impressive, blooming from April through June. These waxy flowers may easily be a foot in diameter and are delightfully fragrant. Rose-colored fruits, borne on upright stalks, follow the spent flowers.

The fall color is a soft yellow that fades to parchment; then the leaves fall to the ground. The dried fallen leaves are attractive in their own right. The bark of the tree is smooth and the branching is sparse. In winter, the thick twigs have a knobby look.

Bigleaf magnolia may reach 40 feet tall with a spreading crown of 20 to 30 feet across. In spite of the big leaves, the crown is very open because of sparse lateral branching, but it is not unusual for the tree to grow multiple trunks.

## In the Landscape

Bigleaf magnolia's exotic look makes it effective in any location in need of an eye-catching tree. Plant it beside a path to enjoy the shade of the massive leaves or in front of a wall to silhouette the trunk. Because of its open branching, the tree's winter form has sharply defined lines. This tree is excellent for rapid deciduous screening in shady, moist locations.

## Planting and Care

Shelter bigleaf magnolia from wind gusts because the leaves will tear easily. Plant in moist, slightly acid soil that is rich in organic matter. Bigleaf magnolia will grow in sun or shade. However, the summer heat of the South is hard on the tree.

## Other Species

There are several other large-leafed magnolias that are similar to bigleaf magnolia but vary slightly in size, range, or growth habit.

Ashe magnolia *(Magnolia ashei)* is native to the lower South and has smaller leaves and a more shrublike form than bigleaf magnolia. It seldom grows more than 20 feet tall. Fraser magnolia, *(Magnolia fraseri),* also a Southern native, has smaller leaves. Its

*The flowers of the native deciduous magnolias have a grace that matches the exotic foliage.*

AT A GLANCE

## BIGLEAF MAGNOLIA
*Magnolia macrophylla*

**Features:** very large leaves, white flowers

**Foliage:** deciduous

**Outstanding season:** summer

**Height:** 30 to 40 feet

**Spread:** 20 feet

**Growth rate:** moderate

**Native:** yes

**Range:** Zones 5 to 9

**Light:** full sun to partial shade

**Pests:** none specific

**Remarks:** subject to heat stress in southern part of range

*The tulip-shaped, upright flowers of lily magnolia open just in advance of the emerging foliage.*

leaves vary from 8 to 15 inches in length and its fragrant blooms may be 9 inches in diameter. This tree is often difficult to distinguish from ashe magnolia; however, its glossy buds have a tinge of purple while the buds of ashe magnolia do not.

Umbrella magnolia *(Magnolia tripetala)* looks very much like bigleaf magnolia but seldom grows more than 30 to 40 feet tall. Its leaves, which may be 2 feet long, are clustered near the ends of the branches, giving the impression of a parasol.

The leaves of cucumber magnolia *(Magnolia acuminata)* are only 4 to 10 inches long; its blooms have greenish-yellow petals and are not highly valued. Though it appears to be compact when young, it will eventually grow to 60 feet tall and equally wide. This tree is hardy from Zones 3 to 8 but will grow only in rich, well-drained, acid soil and will not tolerate extreme heat or cold.

# Lily Magnolia

Lily magnolia blooms in spring, just as its foliage is developing, and has the deepest color of the Oriental magnolias. Its blooms are purplish red with a contrasting white interior and look like tulips on the ends of the branches. The flowers have a slight watermelon fragrance. In fall the leaves turn yellow; winter reveals the silvery-gray bark and the large, almost fuzzy buds that are characteristic of all magnolias.

Lily magnolia grows slowly to 8 to 12 feet in both height and spread. Its size and open branching habit make it nearly shrublike, so that the flowers are generally carried at eye level. This can be used in places where you want to plant a colorful, flowering tree but overhead power lines or other height restrictions prohibit taller plants.

*Slow growing and shrublike, lily magnolia looks best with a dark backdrop that contrasts with its light bark and single flowers.*

# In the Landscape

The slight stature and open branching habit of lily magnolia make it a choice tree for foundation plantings. You can plant lily magnolia in any location that will silhouette its branching form, prominent buds, and showy flowers. Dark backdrops, such as dark brick or the shade of existing woods, highlight the plant's light green foliage.

Use this tree in a border or at the edge of a lawn where it will highlight garden architecture, such as a bench or a birdbath, and then gracefully blend into the background. Lily magnolia will also work well in a courtyard or in an old-fashioned flower garden that is framed by a picket fence. It is a manageable choice for small spaces.

# Planting and Care

Plant lily magnolia in slightly acid, well-drained soil that is rich in organic matter. It will survive in full sun or partial shade but will bloom best if it receives at least four to six hours of direct sun.

Lily magnolia blooms later than other Oriental magnolias and is less likely to be damaged by a cold snap. As with any Oriental magnolia, you may further ensure its success by planting it on the north or northeast side of buildings where early spring sun will not coax it into bloom prematurely.

# Different Selections

Nigra is a selection with 5-inch flowers that are darker colored and bloom later than the species. O'Neill has similar flowers and is noted for its vigor.

A group of hybrids, developed at the National Arboretum and often called the "little girl" hybrids, are crosses between lily magnolia and star magnolia. These bloom even later than the parents, so they are less susceptible to frost damage. They include Ann, Betty, Susan, Jane, and Judy, among others. Their blooms are shades of purple on the outside with a white or pink blush on the inside.

# Saucer Magnolia

Saucer magnolia is the most spectacular and the most popular of the Oriental magnolias, growing 20 to 30 feet tall and nearly as wide. Huge cup-shaped flowers are 5 to 10 inches across and are typically bicolored—white on the inside and pink, rose, or purplish red on the outside. Large foliage gives the tree a coarse texture, and the fall color is medium brown.

*The huge blossoms of saucer magnolia are typically flushed pink or purplish-red on the outside and nearly white inside.*

## AT A GLANCE
❖
## SAUCER MAGNOLIA
*Magnolia* x *soulangiana*

**Features:** outstanding large flowers
**Foliage:** deciduous
**Outstanding season:** winter, spring
**Height:** 20 to 30 feet
**Spread:** 20 to 30 feet
**Growth rate:** moderate to rapid
**Native:** no
**Range:** Zones 4 to 9
**Light:** full sun to partial shade
**Pests:** none specific
**Remarks:** blooms may be damaged by late freezes

*Saucer magnolia is one of the showiest of all flowering trees and needs a prominent space to display its abundant blooms.*

While saucer magnolia typically has a multitrunked form with smooth gray bark, it grows differently in response to local climate. The cooler climates of Kentucky, northern Virginia, and northward slow its growth rate to moderate and the tree develops an exceptionally sculptural form. In the deep South, saucer magnolia grows rapidly to become a stately small shade tree.

## In the Landscape

Saucer magnolia should be planted as an open-lawn specimen or at the junction of a driveway and the street. This tree is too big for foundation plantings, although it may be planted about 15 feet from the house as an accent.

Three trees make an effective cluster in the open lawn, especially when underplanted with a colorful mixture of flowering plants, such as daffodils and periwinkle. Since saucer magnolias drop both large petals and seedpods, they do not work well beside patios.

In the lower South, where growth is more vigorous, saucer magnolia can be used as the corner anchor of a large garden or the focal tree beside a driveway. It will be shown off splendidly against the dark background of an evergreen screen or as a border specimen beneath the canopy of large trees.

In the northern parts of its hardiness range, the striking form of the tree should be highlighted by a backdrop, such as a garden wall or the side of a garage.

## Planting and Care

Saucer magnolias do well in full sun but the filtered noon shade of high pines or willow oaks is better. Planting in partial shade will delay premature blooming. Plant in deep, rich, slightly acid soil with plenty of organic matter. Saucer magnolia needs well-drained soil and constant moisture during the heat of summer.

The tree heals slowly from pruning cuts, so do not prune unless absolutely necessary. If you must prune, the best time to do so is immediately after spring flowering.

## Different Selections

The different selections of saucer magnolia have different blooming patterns. Alexandrina has deep rose-purple petals that are white inside; this selection is the first saucer magnolia to bloom, which makes it susceptible to damage in areas prone to late freezes. Brozzonii bears 10-inch flowers and is the last to bloom. Verbanica is also a late-blooming selection and has rose-colored petals that are white inside; Lennei has dark purplish-magenta blooms.

# Star Magnolia

Star magnolia, named for its star-shaped blooms, is one of the first magnolias to bloom each year, opening its large buds with the daffodils and the forsythia. It is also one of the smallest, slowly growing to 10 to 15 feet in both height and spread.

The fragrant white flowers are 3 to 4 inches across and have 9 to 18 petals radiating from a slightly yellow center. These flowers do not last more than 5 days; fortunately, the buds open at different times, making the flowering show longer. The individual leaves are 2 to 4 inches long and densely cover the small tree. The leaves turn a lovely yellow bronze in fall.

## In the Landscape

Star magnolia's diminutive size and shrubby growth habit make it a versatile plant to use in small gardens or in foundation plantings. The branch structure is informal and slightly irregular, but the plant is very neat, making it an excellent choice for the narrow space beside entry steps or in a border beside a wall. Star magnolia also works well at the junction of a sidewalk and a driveway or in elevated planters as a patio accent.

*All of the flowers do not open at once, so star magnolia has a lengthy period of bloom.*

AT A GLANCE
❖
### STAR MAGNOLIA
*Magnolia stellata*

**Features:** early flowers, shrubby form
**Foliage:** deciduous
**Outstanding season:** early spring
**Height:** 10 to 15 feet
**Spread:** 10 to 15 feet
**Growth rate:** slow
**Native:** no
**Range:** Zones 3 to 8
**Light:** full sun to partial shade
**Pests:** none specific
**Remarks:** subject to damage from late freezes

*Star magnolia is one of the first magnolias to bloom.*

In winter, the large buds and twiggy form provide a subtle ornamental effect that is nicely silhouetted against a solid background of evergreens, a privacy fence, or an entry wall.

## Planting and Care

Like most magnolias, star magnolia likes moist, well-drained, acid soil. It will grow in full sun or in shade, but plants in full sun are more likely to bloom prematurely, thus increasing their risk of damage by a late-spring freeze.

Plant star magnolia on the north or northeast side of the garden to slow down its rush to bloom. Its eagerness to flower (sometimes as early as February in the deep South) puts it in jeopardy of damage from a freeze.

## Different Selections

Three excellent star magnolia selections are Centennial, with large white flowers flushed with pink, Royal Star, with extra-large pure white flowers, and Rubra, with purplish-rose flowers.

## Loebner Magnolia

Loebner magnolia is a profusely flowering hybrid that at first glance is frequently thought to be star magnolia, one of its parent plants. Loebner magnolia has larger flowers than star magnolia; like star magnolia, the flowers of Loebner magnolia have narrow petals that are 2 to 2½ inches long and fragrant.

This is a vigorous, fast-growing hybrid that will reach 25 feet in height and equal spread with a rounded to broad-rounded form. Its bark is light gray and smooth in texture and its branching is dense.

## In the Landscape

Loebner magnolia needs plenty of room to grow. Plant it as a specimen in the open lawn or at the junction of two paths or a path and a driveway. You may substitute Loebner magnolia for dogwoods in planting sites that are very hot and sunny. Avoid using Loebner magnolia for foundation plantings unless you plant it far enough away from the house (at least 15 feet) to give it sufficient room to grow. In informal landscapes, Loebner magnolia works well in garden borders beneath the shade of high canopy trees or clustered in an open lawn.

---

**AT A GLANCE**

❖

### LOEBNER MAGNOLIA
*Magnolia* x *loebneri*

**Features:** profuse flowers, vigorous growth

**Foliage:** deciduous

**Outstanding season:** spring

**Height:** 25 to 30 feet

**Spread:** 25 to 30 feet

**Growth rate:** moderate to rapid

**Native:** no

**Range:** Zones 4 to 9

**Light:** sun to partial shade

**Pests:** none specific

**Remarks:** one of the fastest growing magnolias

## Planting and Care

Loebner magnolia will take full sun but prefers filtered afternoon shade. Planting in partial shade will help prevent the tree from blooming prematurely. Plant in rich, slightly acid soil that is rich in organic matter. Excellent drainage is a must, as is regular watering during summer.

## Different Selections

Merrill, also called Dr. Merrill, is a vigorous, freely blooming plant with 3- to 3½-inch flowers that are white with a blotch of pink at the base. Other selections include Leonard Messel, with white petals that have a rose-pink stripe, and Spring Snow, with late, fragrant flowers.

# Yulan Magnolia

Yulan magnolia, a parent plant of saucer magnolia, may be the ultimate tree for collectors, as it is one of the oldest cultivated magnolias. This tree graced temple gardens in ancient China and was first grown in Europe in the late 18th century. It grows to tremendous size, reaching 30 to 40 feet in both height and spread, and resembles saucer magnolia in form and landscape uses.

Yulan magnolia blooms very early, just after star magnolia. The pure white flowers have nine petals and are upright and tulip shaped. They are also extremely fragrant.

## In the Landscape

Yulan magnolia should be used as an open-lawn specimen or as an accent plant in a garden border because it is massive enough to stand alone. It is too large to work in most foundation plantings or under power lines but can be silhouetted against a garage or other structure.

## Planting and Care

Plant yulan magnolia in slightly acid soil that is rich in organic matter. The flowers may be damaged by sudden cold snaps, so plant it on the north or northeast side of the residence to thwart its natural rush to bloom prematurely.

Yulan magnolia may be difficult to locate in garden centers, but it is worth the search if you have a spot for a very large tree with fragrant flowers.

*Yulan magnolia is one of the oldest cultivated magnolias.*

### AT A GLANCE
❖

### YULAN MAGNOLIA
*Magnolia heptapeta*

**Features:** fragrant white flowers

**Foliage:** deciduous

**Outstanding season:** spring

**Height:** 30 to 40 feet

**Spread:** 30 to 40 feet

**Growth rate:** moderate

**Native:** no

**Range:** Zones 5 to 9

**Light:** partial shade

**Pests:** none specific

**Remarks:** subject to damage from late freezes

# Maple

*Japanese maples are prized for their superior fall color, which may be yellow, orange, or red, depending on the selection.*

Maples are some of the most satisfactory and widely planted shade trees for many reasons: they are free of debilitating diseases and insect pests, they adapt well to a variety of horticultural conditions, and they provide reliable shade and splendid fall color. What's more, you can enjoy the results of planting a maple in less than a lifetime.

In warmer climates, maples grow quickly; they rapidly become effective in the landscape with no sacrifice in hardiness or longevity. These plants also have a remarkable tolerance for varying soil conditions. Only the severe heat of south Florida, the Gulf Coast, and south Texas diminishes the dependability of some species.

While sugar maple and red maple are native throughout the entire Eastern United States, they are generally considered a northern species because of their blazing autumn color in New England. However, these trees grow naturally in hardwood forests throughout the Mid-Atlantic and South as well, and their fall color is every bit as reliable, if not as vivid, as that of their New England counterparts.

## A Closer Look

The hallmark of maples is their fall color, which ranges in hue from silver maple's lemon yellow to the flame orange of sugar maple to the ruby red of red maple. Typically, the color will vary widely within a species—even among the leaves of a single tree—and to some degree with the latitude of the planting, the higher latitudes having more brilliant color.

While the autumn show is reason enough to select a maple, these trees offer many other attributes that provide ornamental appeal throughout the entire year. As a genus, maples are one of the few large deciduous trees that have a noticeable flowering show. They are also some of the earliest trees to bloom. Red maple blooms well in advance of spring, sometimes as early as February in the deep South; it is quickly followed by silver maple and sugar maple.

The flowers are followed by seedpods or **_samaras,_** the familiar maple "wings" that spin playfully to the ground when ripened. These develop quickly, almost imperceptibly, after the flowers and from a distance seem to be a continuation of the blooms. As the new foliage emerges and matures, the samaras begin fluttering to the ground.

*Winged seeds called* samaras *are characteristic of maples and appear before the foliage.*

The leaves quickly follow the samaras. They unfold with a slight blush of color, nearly mauve, before assuming a bright, fresh green that darkens to the characteristic medium green of the growing season. Silver maple is the exception to the maple's generally steady green; its leaves have lighter undersides.

Following the autumn show, each maple brings a distinctive form and bark texture to the winter garden. These patterns are not only distinctive enough to be of ornamental value but can also serve as a means of identification.

## In the Landscape

Maples are valued for both shade and show. Except for the small Japanese maple, which has its own landscape uses, maples grow large enough to be excellent primary shade trees, grown either as specimens in the open lawn or in a large mulched bed. They can also be grouped in clusters. Plant maples on the south or southwest side of the house, at least 20 feet from the structure, to allow them to provide good shade.

Plan to use mulch or a vigorous ground cover beneath a maple as these trees have extensive, shallow root systems. In heavy clay soil, the roots tend to grow just below the surface and may even break through, causing grass to grow unevenly and making mowing difficult.

On a treeless lot, a grouping of maples is not only an investment in shade but begins to shape the garden with seasonal interest. Maples naturalize well in existing mulched beds or natural areas and may be planted in informal groups. Because of this, they are superb trees to use for "residential reforestation" on lots where all trees were cleared during construction.

*The largest Japanese maples serve as small, long-lived shade trees. This one becomes a dominant landscape feature in the fall.*

*The foliage of red maple is light green, and the bark is almost silver with mottled patches.*

AT A GLANCE
❖
## RED MAPLE
*Acer rubrum*

**Features:** rapid growth, splendid color, trouble free

**Foliage:** deciduous

**Outstanding season:** fall

**Height:** 40 to 60 feet

**Spread:** 40 to 60 feet

**Growth rate:** moderate to rapid

**Native:** yes

**Range:** Zones 3 to 9

**Light:** full sun

**Pests:** aphids

**Remarks:** Autumn Flame, October Glory, and Red Sunset are the best selections for fall color

If you are fortunate to have existing trees, blend maples into the mix to provide a punch of bright fall color. There is no finer backdrop for maples than pines. Plant red maple in front of loblolly pine; use sugar maple if your property has white pines—the yellow fall color of sugar maple nicely complements the bluish-green cast of white pine.

# Troubleshooting

Maples may be bothered by aphids. These pests suck sap from young leaves and stems and must be controlled. Turn to page 124 for more about aphids.

# Red Maple

This shade tree takes its name from the early flowers it brings to the waning winter landscape. In a gray time of year, red maple becomes a wash of deep red flowers. The blooms are grouped in clusters of as many as 20, delicately suspended on long, red stalks. The samaras are also bright red, extending the color show at least another week.

This medium-sized tree grows rapidly to a mature height of 40 to 60 feet with an equal spread. The leaves have a slightly lighter color on the underside than the characteristic deep green. The tree casts a light shade that permits grass to grow right up to the base of the trunk. In fall, the leaves turn a brilliant red; even in the lower and coastal South, where color change is usually minimal, red maple puts on a glorious show.

Red maple shows another fine characteristic in winter; its smooth, silver-gray bark. In older trees, the bark of the trunk is rough and striated while the upper branches are shiny, light colored, and smooth. This combination aids in identification.

*Red maples are easily identifiable in winter because they have lighter bark than other maples.*

*Red maple, shown here in early spring, has terrific color year-round.*

# In the Landscape

Red maple will work in any garden scheme, whether as a formal shade planting in a row in front of the house, an informal drift along one side of the garden, or loosely incorporated into the garden border. It is as natural along the edge of the driveway as it is at the edge of existing woods or even when used as a free-standing specimen.

Use red maple as the primary shade tree for a house on a treeless lot. Plant it on the south or southwest side of the residence at least 20 feet from the building. Beware of its vigorous root system; red maple should not be planted where it will obstruct septic systems.

# Planting and Care

Red maple grows rapidly and is very tolerant of a wide range of soil conditions. It will grow in soggy soil and does well when planted near a stream or lake. Though it does not mind alkaline soil, it will grow best in rich, slightly acid soil.

*The samaras of red maple quickly follow the flowers and seem to extend the flowering show.*

# Different Selections

Autumn Flame has excellent, early fall color. October Glory is a fast-growing tree that drops its leaves very late in the season but is rather unpredictable; Red Sunset, one of the best for both fall color and hardiness, is a preferred selection.

*The uniform shape of sugar maple lends itself to repetition, such as this planting along a country lane.*

# Sugar Maple

Sugar maple is synonymous with fall color in much of the country and is certainly one of the most widely planted shade trees. The quality of its fall show is better than that of any other maple, and its deep green foliage during the growing season is lovely in itself. The fall color of sugar maples often varies from yellow to orange because of the genetic variations in the seeds from which they sprout. However, named selections have more consistent color.

Sugar maple is nearly unsurpassable as a shade tree if you have both the time and the room for it to mature. Older specimen trees can be 80 feet tall with a 40- to 50-foot spread. The bark of older trees is coarse, rugged, and slightly shaggy, similar to that of white oak.

One of the most unusual and delightful characteristics of sugar maple is the way it drops its brilliant-colored leaves in the fall, from the top of the tree down. The branches of the upper portion of the tree will emerge from a girdle of brilliant leaves still clinging below.

The crown is upright and rounded, sometimes branching low from the trunk, and is quite suitable for climbing. A healthy tree throws a dark shadow, making it difficult to establish a thick turf beneath the canopy.

## In the Landscape

Select sugar maple as your primary shade tree for the open lawn. Its uniform, lollipop shape lends itself to straightforward planting schemes; use sugar maples as street trees or pair them on opposite sides of a sidewalk. Use sugar maple to line a lengthy driveway or to outline a rectangular, treeless lot. It will also do quite well as a specimen tree planted in the yard of an L-shaped house.

## Planting and Care

Sugar maple prefers moist, acid soil. It does not do well in soggy soil or compacted clay, nor is it tolerant of hot, polluted conditions, which will scorch the leaves. It needs room to spread its roots.

---

AT A GLANCE
❖
## SUGAR MAPLE
*Acer saccharum*

**Features:** deep shade, predictable shape, glorious fall color

**Foliage:** deciduous

**Outstanding season:** summer, fall

**Height:** 60 to 75 feet, sometimes 100 feet

**Spread:** 40 to 50 feet

**Growth rate:** slow

**Native:** yes

**Range:** Zones 4 to 8

**Light:** full sun

**Pests:** aphids

**Remarks:** one of the best all-around trees

## Species and Selections

Green Mountain is a selection that is more heat tolerant than most sugar maples, although it is not as heat tolerant as Southern sugar maple. Goldspire is a columnar tree with leaves that are less likely to scorch in the peak of a Southern summer. Legacy is a proven selection that is also more heat and drought tolerant than most sugar maples.

Southern sugar maple *(Acer barbatum),* a similar species, offers the lower and coastal South rich fall color like that of sugar maple. Smaller both in leaf and height (25 to 30 feet), Southern sugar maple has a more open habit of growth and is more adapted to the alkaline soil and low, wet sites of coastal areas.

# Silver Maple

Silver maple grows the fastest of all popular maples, racing to 70 feet in height with a spread of 35 to 50 feet. Its name comes from the color of the undersides of the deeply cut leaves; when a breeze stirs silver maple, the tree seems to shimmer. In fall, the tree turns lemon yellow. In winter, the shaggy bark, which is silver gray with light brown highlights, is its most ornamental feature.

# In the Landscape

Many homeowners and landscape professionals are not fond of silver maple because its rapid growth often results in weak wood. While this makes it susceptible to wind or ice damage, the tree does have limited uses.

If you have sudden need for a privacy screen on a large property, silver maple is a good tree to plant to create a living veil. The key is to limit your use of silver maple to areas where it will cause no damage to your property if split in a storm.

Compared to other maples, silver maple is a short-lived tree. However, it is a better choice than other fast-growing trees, such as poplar, for quickly filling a gap until long-lived trees mature.

# Planting and Care

Silver maple will adapt to any soil condition, from sandy loam to heavy clay, and it tolerates alkaline soil. Plant it in full sun for the best growth. Silver maple will tolerate shade but as it is a shade tree, you do not need to plant it if you have a shady garden.

*The glowing yellow leaves of sugar maple retain their color as they carpet the ground with gold.*

AT A GLANCE
❖
## SILVER MAPLE
*Acer saccharinum*

**Features:** open crown, leaves have silver undersides
**Foliage:** deciduous
**Outstanding season:** fall
**Height:** 50 to 70 feet
**Spread:** 35 to 50 feet
**Growth rate:** rapid
**Native:** yes
**Range:** Zones 3 to 9
**Light:** full sun to partial shade
**Pests:** aphids
**Remarks:** more susceptible to disease and wind damage than other maples

*The finely textured leaves of cutleaf Japanese maples are prized for their softness.*

## AT A GLANCE
❖
## JAPANESE MAPLE
*Acer palmatum*

**Features:** exquisite foliage, artful form

**Foliage:** deciduous

**Outstanding season:** all seasons

**Height:** 3 to 30 feet

**Spread:** 2 to 20 feet

**Growth rate:** full range

**Native:** no

**Range:** Zones 5 to 8

**Light:** full sun to partial shade

**Pests:** aphids

**Remarks:** one of the finest small trees for fall color

# Japanese Maple

Landscape designers describe Japanese maple as a four-season tree for its year-round beauty. Because of its smaller stature, it is closer to eye level than other maples, making the tree an excellent selection for a patio or a terrace planting. Some selections of Japanese maple can be maintained at 36 inches tall; others may shoot to more than 30 feet. This is one of the best trees for an entry or courtyard accent because it is beautifully dressy throughout the year. Even in winter, the tree's form and colorful twigs make it an eye-catching contribution to the garden.

Some selections have purple or bronze leaves throughout the growing season and should be carefully placed as accents in the garden. Without question, the fall color of the green-leafed selections exceeds any other tree species in quality, variety, and reliability. Usually among the last to change color, the bright leaves of Japanese maple glow when backlit by the setting autumn sun. These leaves look like an open hand that is ***dissected,*** or divided, into 5 to 11 "fingers" or lobes. The depth of dissection and the length and width of the lobes depend on the selection. This airy, intricate foliage is embroidery in the landscape.

## Different Selections

Japanese maples are divided into six groups—palmate, dissectum, deeply divided, dwarf, variegated, and special feature. The names of the first three refer to the shape of the leaves. The differences are not always evident to less experienced buyers but are important to know, as there is a significant range in price, growth rate, and mature size.

Trees in the palmate group, which includes the parent species, are mostly upright, growing 10 to 30 feet tall. Leaves may be red, green, or purple.

Selections in the dissectum category are also known as splitleaf or cutleaf maples. These trees feature cascading branches, grow broader than tall, and usually reach 6 to 10 feet in height. Their fine, filigreed leaves may be red, bronze, or green and give the tree a lacy texture. The best-known tree in this group is threadleaf Japanese maple, which has deeply dissected leaves with extremely thin, delicate lobes. Some specimens of this plant have reached only 4 feet in height even after 50 years of growth.

Deeply divided maples have characteristics between the palmate and dissectum types and may have varying foliage colors. Burgundy Lace is one such selection with a deep wine red color in early spring that changes to a greenish burgundy for the summer.

Members of the dwarf group slowly grow to 6 feet or less in height. These plants are prized as bonsai trees and for use as accent plantings.

The variegated group consists of trees with several different foliage colors on one plant. These variegated trees are specialty plants and are often hard to find in garden centers. Look for them in mail-order catalogs.

Trees in the special features group possess an unusual trait that makes them exceptional. For example, a selection named Sango Kaku sports bright red bark.

# In the Landscape

Because of its many shapes, sizes, and colors, Japanese maple presents a number of design possibilities. Dwarf and dissectum types are best for containers because of their limited size. You may also inter-plant Japanese maples with small shrubs and perennials as part of a border. The tree's color and texture enhance the seasonal nature of a well-planned border.

While the upright, spreading growth habit is pleasing from a distance, the intricacy of the foliage, the texture of the bark, and the delicacy of the twigs are best appreciated at close range. In this respect, Japanese maples are excellent small shade trees for court-yards and terraces.

Japanese maples work well beside an entry or near a window because of their year-round attributes. Also, the root system is not invasive and the mature size is small, which means that the tree can be used as close as 8 feet to the house. The light branches will not damage stucco or other soft surfaces if the wind whips the limbs against it. The plant responds well to careful pruning, which makes it well adapted to small, tight landscape situations.

# Planting and Care

While Japanese maples can grow in direct summer sun, the tree does best if provided three to four hours of filtered shade daily. This is par-ticularly true of the small-leafed types. Moist, well-drained soil that is neutral or slightly acid is best. Japanese maples are long-lived trees if provided proper care. Be sure to keep them sufficiently watered during periods of drought.

*Japanese maple is one of the best trees for small courtyards, where all of its attributes are easily observed.*

*You must view Japanese maple up close to appreciate its smooth bark and beauti-ful branch structure.*

# Oak

*The upright form and small leaves of willow oak allow sunlight to penetrate beneath older trees to allow grass to grow.*

Oaks command respect and draw affection that is accorded no other trees; they are landmarks, old friends, and living shelters. In the garden or in their native woods, oaks provide a welcome shade and a sense of place.

Part of the mystique of oaks comes from their longevity—individual trees can be far older than the owner of the land they shade. Oaks withstand natural calamities, such as storms and fires, better than most other trees, and their wood possesses uncommon strength and durability. When you choose an oak for your garden, you are bequeathing its majesty to generations yet to come.

## A Closer Look

You are probably aware that there are many different kinds of oak trees growing within an acorn's toss of your home. Many species are native to each region of the country, though few are restricted to that one area. These native trees have few limitations of soil or geography; only the majestic live oak of the lower and coastal South is restricted in its adaptability. Most oaks can tolerate wide variance in temperature and are not particular about whether the soil is sandy, well drained, or thick with clay. This adaptability means you have many choices when selecting an oak for your garden.

While maples generally surpass oaks in fall color, oaks make better lawn and street trees because they have a deeper root system and a higher, stronger canopy. They typically offer more open shade, which allows sunlight to filter lightly through. No group of trees rivals oaks for the hardiness, the utility, and the majesty that they bring to the garden.

Oaks have a reputation for being slow-growing trees, but this is not true of them all. White oak and live oak do take considerable time to reach their celebrated stature, growing less than a foot per year. Other oaks, notably red oak, pin oak, and willow oak, easily grow at twice that rate, particularly when young. Willow oak can be expected to gain an inch in trunk diameter each growing season.

## In the Landscape

One or two mature oaks can easily shade a lawn, a terrace, or even the entire house. If your lot has few trees, plant oaks to shade the south and west sides of your property but do not plant them any closer than 20 feet to your home. This minimum distance allows the tree to develop a sturdy root system without pressuring the foundation of the house and will also reduce the number of *tassels* (male flowers) and acorns that drop into your gutters.

You should also plant oaks at least 20 feet from a patio, a sidewalk, or a driveway. Otherwise, you will see damage as the tree grows; its roots will spread, buckling the pavement.

All oaks produce acorns—a consideration if you plan to use them as the shade trees for a driveway or a patio. The sound of acorns falling on a new car may not be music to your ears! Also, fallen acorns will sprout if left uncollected; if you do not rake them, plan to weed seedlings.

Use a combination of several oaks to establish a natural area in the lawn. As these trees mature and cast shade, they will create a new range of horticultural conditions beneath their canopies. Such plantings also provide the natural conditions favored by wildlife.

If you are building on property with existing oaks, you must manage the construction sequence carefully to preserve the trees. Refer to pages 36–37 for more on careful construction.

# Live Oak

Although it grows rapidly in early years, live oak takes decades to achieve its majestic stature, with branches as stout as trunks. If you have a mature live oak on your property, consider yourself fortunate.

The leaves of live oak are 2 to 4 inches long, ½ to 2 inches wide, smooth, and shiny black green during the growing season. The tree is considered evergreen because the leaves remain on the tree until new spring growth pushes them off, with little or no color change at all.

In areas of high humidity and rainfall, the tree attains its classic form: a short, massive trunk with huge, sprawling limbs, the lowest of which sweep the ground. In the dry hills and plains of the Southwest, live oak looks entirely different, becoming gnarled and almost stunted, growing one-half its potential size. Wherever it grows, live oak casts a deep but mottled shade.

## In the Landscape

Live oak is a specimen tree for a patient gardener with a lot of room and plenty of time. Use live oak either as an open-lawn specimen or to provide shade for a driveway. Plant live oaks on either side of a long driveway; place them 60 feet apart and at least 20 feet from the pavement.

*In arid parts of Texas, live oaks develop a gnarly character, just as they do when used as a shield against salt spray.*

**AT A GLANCE**

❖

### LIVE OAK
*Quercus virginiana*

**Features:** magnificent shade
**Foliage:** evergreen
**Outstanding season:** spring
**Height:** 40 to 80 feet
**Spread:** 60 to 100 feet
**Growth rate:** moderate
**Native:** yes
**Range:** Zones 8 to 10
**Light:** full sun
**Pests:** none specific
**Remarks:** slow growing but worth the wait

*Pin oak has a well-defined pyramidal form.*

## AT A GLANCE
❖
## PIN OAK
*Quercus palustris*

**Features:** pyramidal shape,
good fall color
**Foliage:** deciduous
**Outstanding season:** fall
**Height:** 60 to 70 feet
**Spread:** 25 to 40 feet
**Growth rate:** fast
**Native:** yes
**Range:** Zones 4 to 8
**Light:** full sun
**Pests:** none specific
**Remarks:** one of the fastest
growing oaks

Live oaks may be planted to create a buffer from salt spray, which will deform the tree into a sculpted, weathered form that is quite striking. In arid climates, such as Texas, group young live oaks intentionally close together to force them to reach for light. This will cause their trunks to lean and and will provide shade within the landscape.

## Planting and Care

Live oak will grow in just about any soil—wet, dry, acid, alkaline, sand, clay, even silt. The most vigorous growth, however, occurs when the tree is planted in rich, well-drained soil.

This tree is a vigorous feeder and, when mature, casts a deep shade, making it difficult to grow a lawn beneath the canopy. Plan to use a ground cover, or mulch around the base as the tree matures.

## Pin Oak

Pin oak brings several attributes to the landscape that make it a popular oak. It has unusual form, good fall color, dependable cold hardiness, and pest resistance. The tree is rigidly pyramidal, and when it is young, the lower branches slant to the ground. The form changes very little as the tree grows to its mature height of 60 to 70 feet with a spread of 25 to 40 feet.

The glossy, green leaves are 4 to 6 inches long and are deeply lobed. The characteristic U-shaped lobes taper to sharp points. In fall, the leaves turn russet, bronze, or orange red. The leaves do not fall quickly but hang on the tree throughout the winter. While this is a beautiful effect, the leaves eventually drop in early spring; the litter of dead leaves can be a nuisance if the tree is planted near a patio.

## In the Landscape

Pin oak, with its predictable, rigid form, is a good choice if you need an oak with uniform shape. The tree looks best in formal uses when repeated several times, such as in rows along a drive, as a street tree, or in a row across the front of your property. Remove the downward-slanting lower limbs that interfere with walking if you use it as a street tree or to shade a driveway or a sidewalk.

It is moderately effective as a single specimen because the dried foliage remains through the winter. Groups of pin oak in an informal bed can be very effective to shape space within a lawn.

*A trio of oaks shows the variety of oak's fall color.* (From left: *red oak, willow oak, pin oak*)

# Planting and Care

Pin oak will do well in full sun or partial shade. It tolerates varying soil conditions; in the wild it grows in wet clay. Pin oak does best in moist, rich, well-drained, acid soil and may not do well in the alkaline soils of the Midwest, Arkansas, Oklahoma, and Texas. Here it may become chlorotic; the leaves will yellow. It prefers the cooler parts of its range and is not recommended for the lower and coastal South.

# Troubleshooting

Yellowing of the foliage may indicate chlorosis, which can seriously damage the tree. This is a difficult condition to overcome; treating the tree and its surrounding soil with a spray of liquid iron will help correct the problem.

# Different Selections

Sovereign is a selection with low branches held at a 45- to 90-degree angle from the main trunk; Crown Rite is similar in form, though more narrow through the crown.

# Red Oak

Red oak, sometimes called Northern red oak, is another excellent, fast-growing oak. This native tree prefers the cool climates of the higher latitudes of its range but will also grow in the middle South.

---

AT A GLANCE
❖
## RED OAK
*Quercus rubra*

**Features:** fast growing, good fall color
**Foliage:** deciduous
**Outstanding season:** fall
**Height:** 60 to 75 feet
**Spread:** 40 to 50 feet
**Growth rate:** fast
**Native:** yes
**Range:** Zones 4 to 8
**Light:** full sun to partial shade
**Pests:** none specific
**Remarks:** a cold-hardy, well-shaped oak

*The brilliant red fall color and C-shaped lobes are characteristic of scarlet oak.*

Red oak has a rounded crown when young that becomes more open as it matures to its 60- to 75-foot height. The leaves are about 9 inches long with 7 to 11 lobes that taper to sharp bristles. The foliage is almost mauve when it first emerges, turning lustrous dark green during the growing season and then russet to bright red in fall.

The bark has flat, gray patches intermingled with ridged and darker furrowed areas that look like vertical banding. This is one of the best keys for identification.

## In the Landscape

Red oak holds its lower branches directly out from the trunk, making it a better choice than pin oak for a street tree or for shading a driveway. The upright, rounded crown also makes it an excellent open-lawn specimen.

Use red oak as one component of a fall-color composition in the garden border, planting it with another fast-growing tree, such as sugar maple, that will turn yellow in fall.

## Planting and Care

Red oak likes rich sandy loam that is well drained and slightly acid. It does not do well in alkaline soils. Though it will grow in Zone 8, red oak will do better when planted north of the line from Little Rock to Birmingham to Atlanta.

## Scarlet Oak

Scarlet oak is often confused with pin oak, but its leaves have noticeable C-shaped, bristle-tipped lobes and are wider in the middle than those of pin oak. The foliage is glossy, lustrous green on top; the underside is smooth.

Unlike pin oak, which has sharply descending lower branches, scarlet oak holds its branches directly away from the trunk and the top is rounded, not pyramidal. This tree has a more relaxed look than the widely planted pin oak.

## In the Landscape

Although difficult to find in nurseries, scarlet oak is preferable in many ways to pin oak and can serve in many of the same landscape uses. Since its lower branches are held more upright than those of pin oak, it is better for use as a street tree or for shading a driveway. This growth habit makes it easier to mow beneath when the tree is used as an open-lawn specimen. The rounded crown also makes scarlet oak a good choice for naturalizing in a large border.

## Planting and Care

Plant scarlet oak in well-drained, slightly acid soil. It is not a good choice for moist or soggy soils; however, it is more tolerant than pin oak of the alkaline soils of the Midwest, Texas, Arkansas, and Oklahoma. Scarlet oak will withstand drier conditions than pin oak and is less likely to develop chlorosis in alkaline soil.

## Different Selections

The most commonly available selection of scarlet oak is Splendens, which has brilliant long-lasting fall color.

# Shumard Oak

Shumard oak, also called swamp red oak, is a widely distributed and adaptable native tree that will grow in dry or moist, acid or alkaline soil. It grows fairly rapidly to a mature height of 80 to 100 feet or more. Young trees are spreading and rounded, hinting at the almost oval form of a mature tree that can have a 50- to 60-foot spread.

The leaves of Shumard oak are 5 to 8 inches long, 3 to 6 inches wide, and deeply lobed with bristles at the tips of the longest lobes. The leaves, which are reminiscent of red oak, are dark, lustrous green and turn orange red in the fall.

## In the Landscape

Like the other large oaks, Shumard oak is a majestic lawn tree. Its lower branches are held straight out from the trunk, making it easy to walk around the tree when mowing. The upright, rounded crown, which is more casual than the rigid pyramidal form of pin oak, makes it a better tree for informal, natural plantings.

## Planting and Care

Give Shumard oak plenty of sun and a lot of room. It grows best in deep, fertile, well-drained soil but is tolerant of other conditions.

The greatest advantage of Shumard oak is its adaptability to varying soil conditions. Experts cite its tolerance of moist locations and its ability to withstand alkaline soils as strong qualities that earn it an easy-to-grow reputation.

*Shumard oak's upright, oval form and branching habit make it a good choice for lawn specimens and street trees.*

AT A GLANCE
❖
## SHUMARD OAK
*Quercus shumardii*

**Features:** fast growth, rounded form
**Foliage:** deciduous
**Outstanding season:** fall
**Height:** 80 to 100 feet
**Spread:** 50 to 60 feet
**Growth rate:** fast
**Native:** yes
**Range:** Zones 5 to 9
**Light:** full sun
**Pests:** none specific
**Remarks:** one of the best oaks for fall color

*White oak leaves have rounded lobes and turn an intense red in fall.*

## AT A GLANCE

### WHITE OAK
*Quercus alba*

**Features:** massive size, plated bark

**Foliage:** deciduous

**Outstanding season:** summer

**Height:** 70 to 90 feet

**Spread:** 50 to 80 feet

**Growth rate:** slow to medium

**Native:** yes

**Range:** Zones 3 to 9

**Light:** full sun

**Pests:** none specific

**Remarks:** a majestic oak with beautiful bark

# White Oak

The majestic white oak has the same symbolic stature of inland locations that live oak holds in the lower and coastal South. It is a large, spreading tree that grows from a pyramidal form in its youth to become a broad, rounded form that may exceed 90 feet in height with a 50- to 80-foot spread.

The leaves of white oak emerge a pastel red, grow about 4 inches wide and 5 to 9 inches long, and then turn deep blue green. They are lobed with rounded tips and turn russet to rich wine red in fall, holding their color for several weeks. The leaves remain on young trees through winter and then fall continually in spring.

The branches are stout, giving the tree a powerful winter silhouette. The tree's name comes from the light gray bark, which is arranged in vertical strips that look like shingles.

## In the Landscape

Like live oak, white oak is a prized specimen shade tree that grows slowly. It may take 60 years to achieve its full majesty. If you do not have mature white oak trees on your property, do not choose white oak for quick shade or immediate effect. Plant it as a legacy tree in a prominent location, such as on the crown of a hill, in the curve of a lengthy drive, or near the intersection of the driveway and the street. Choose a planting site at least 35 feet from overhead power lines and paved surfaces so that the tree may safely grow without interference.

## Planting and Care

Unfortunately, white oak does not transplant well, and the best chances for success in the home landscape come from planting young (3- to 5-foot-tall), container-grown trees. If you want to transplant a large tree, it will be worth your while to have landscape professionals plant it and provide a guarantee.

Plant white oak in full sun and rich, slightly acid soil. In natural areas, allow the fallen leaves to decay in the tree's feeding area to replenish organic matter and nutrients, and maintain soil acidity.

## Species and Selections

A related oak, swamp white oak *(Quercus bicolor),* has similar bark and may be easier to find in nurseries than white oak. It is native from Quebec to Georgia and is easier to transplant than white oak.

# Willow Oak

If you can plant only one tree to provide shade for both your home and garden, plant a willow oak. This oval tree with its high, arching canopy is considered a fast grower. It reaches 50 to 80 feet at maturity with a 30- to 40-foot spread.

The common name reflects the similarity of the leaves to those of weeping willow. The individual leaves are 3 to 5 inches long, ¼ to ½ inch wide, and lance shaped with smooth edges, making the tree much finer in texture than most oaks. The small leaves and thin twigs give the plant an open, airy appearance.

The tree's fall color varies from yellow to golden brown. The branching habit is open, and the bark is slightly rough on older trees. Willow oak's acorns are small but there are many of them; in spring, they will sprout all over the garden.

## In the Landscape

This tough tree is the preferred street tree of many Southern cities because it tolerates urban conditions, responds well to pruning, and soars to shade a street with its canopy.

Use willow oak as the primary shade tree in your landscape. Two mature trees can easily shade the average yard. The filtered shade cast by willow oak is ideal for bedding plants and shrubs that need protection from the summer sun, such as rhododendrons and azaleas.

## Planting and Care

Willow oak needs full sun and moist, loamy soil that is well drained. It does not do well in alkaline soil; it may develop chlorosis. Thus the plant is not suited to Texas, Oklahoma, or Arkansas.

Willow oak is a vigorous tree and has expansive roots. Avoid planting near septic drain pipes as the roots may block the lines.

*Willow oaks make excellent street trees.*

*Willow oak will become a magnificent open-lawn specimen with a rounded crown.*

AT A GLANCE
❖
## WILLOW OAK
*Quercus phellos*

**Features:** impressive form, good shade
**Foliage:** deciduous
**Outstanding season:** summer
**Height:** 50 to 80 feet
**Spread:** 30 to 40 feet
**Growth rate:** fast
**Native:** yes
**Range:** Zones 7 to 9
**Light:** full sun
**Pests:** none specific
**Remarks:** produces many seedlings

# Pine

*With their lower limbs removed, white pines tower to shade a street.*

Pines play a very important role in the landscape because they are hardy, fast-growing, tall evergreens that are adaptable to varying conditions. Often pines are already present on a property; if not, you should not overlook them as landscape options. Speedy growth is one of their greatest virtues. Most will quickly become stately trees, rivaling Leyland cypress in speed. An 18-inch loblolly pine seedling will exceed 30 feet in 15 years, as will white pine.

Pines are steady in their landscape appeal, beginning in winter when their lustrous green needles provide welcome color to the barren landscape. In spring, the new growth, called *candles,* surges from the tips of the branches to become summer's green foliage. They are steady green during the growing season, with some seasonal yellowing of spent needles in fall. Even young pines, 5 to 10 years old, have great appeal in the landscape as they bear soft green needles before skyrocketing to mature heights.

## In the Landscape

Pines are very hardy plants, performing the thankless tasks of screening unpleasant views, providing shelter from the damaging effects of salt spray, or creating quick shade for ornamental trees. While a well-placed white pine or Japanese black pine makes a noble specimen, most pines are better used in groups. Loblolly pines can create an entire backdrop for the garden. Pines planted as a screen will naturally drop their lower limbs (white pine and Japanese black pine excepted) to create conditions beneath the canopy that will provide a chance for shade-loving ornamentals to thrive.

## Planting and Care

The best way to purchase pines is usually as container-grown plants. Whether you plant a seedling pine, a 4-foot container-grown plant, or a more expensive 8-foot balled-and-burlapped tree, all will be approximately the same size in 5 to 7 years. White pine, however, transplants best as a balled-and-burlapped tree.

Pines need full sun and well-drained soil for best growth but they can tolerate a wide range of soils. White pine is more particular; be sure to plant it in well-drained loamy soil as it does not do well in heavy clay. Japanese black pine adapts well to poor, sandy soils.

When planting a stand of pines, spacing is important. Space loblolly pines 15 feet apart for a fast-growing screen to block an undesirable view. If you live in the mountains or on a large, steep property, plant a zigzag line of white pines with 20 feet between each tree—the trees will "weave" together more gracefully than if planted in a straight line.

If you use pines near a building, plant them at least 20 to 25 feet away so that the lower limbs will not interfere with the building or with pedestrian traffic. Consider staking young trees if you typically have strong prevailing winds.

# Japanese Black Pine

Japanese black pine tolerates cold, heat, and drought, and does well in coastal areas from Florida to New England. This tree is less reliable inland in the northern part of its range. It grows moderately, sometimes rapidly, to a mature height of 20 to 40 feet in most garden settings, although the trees have the capability of reaching 50 feet with a spread of 20 to 30 feet.

The needles, which are stiff to the touch, are about 3 inches long and grow in bundles of two. They maintain their uniform dark green throughout the year; the bark of older trees is black in places, hence the name.

Unlike many other pines, Japanese black pine rarely grows straight; instead, it wanders into an irregular form that becomes bushier with age. Its wayward limbs reach outward from the tree's central trunk.

## In the Landscape

This is a quirky specimen tree that should be silhouetted against a wall or a fence, or used in conjunction with rock or water features. It is a natural plant to use in gardens where a severe, weathered look is preferred. Its drought resistance is useful at the beach, where the tree makes a good salt-tolerant windbreak and dune stabilizer. Japanese black pine provides a slightly exotic look wherever it is planted.

Japanese black pine is one of the only pines that readily adapts to growth in containers and is also popular as a bonsai tree.

## Planting and Care

Japanese black pine needs full sun. It prefers moist, fertile, well-drained soil for the best growth but does adapt well to sandy or clay soils, provided it is well drained.

*Blotchy bark is characteristic of most pines.*

AT A GLANCE
❖
**JAPANESE BLACK PINE**
*Pinus thunbergiana*

**Features:** contorted low branching
**Foliage:** evergreen
**Outstanding season:** all seasons
**Height:** 20 to 50 feet
**Spread:** 20 to 40 feet
**Growth rate:** medium
**Native:** no
**Range:** Zones 5 to 9
**Light:** full sun
**Pests:** none specific
**Remarks:** tolerates salt spray

*The long cones of white pine hang like ornaments.*

# White Pine

White pine finds its way into many homes as a Christmas tree. In the garden, this pine is an excellent large specimen tree, growing fast in the foothills, mountains, and northern latitudes—all cool locations that favor its growth. White pine is native throughout the Eastern United States. It may be planted in the Piedmont, although it sometimes dies mysteriously, perhaps of stress from heat or drought.

White pine maintains a splendid pyramidal form during its youth, becoming somewhat more oval at maturity, with newer, higher branches reaching outward and upward. New needles often have a bluish cast to them, becoming greener during summer. Cones are smooth, grow to about 7 inches long, and hang from the tree like ornaments.

## In the Landscape

White pine will grow 50 to 80 feet tall with a spread of 20 feet in 30 years; in the wild it will soar to 150 feet. Expect the tree to grow 2 feet per year.

Use white pine as a specimen evergreen tree to anchor a corner of the garden. Allow about 20 feet of clearance for the lower branches to spread. Never plant it closer than 20 feet from the house.

On larger properties, white pine can be planted in drifts in an open lawn or used to create a privacy screen. It needs a 20-foot-wide space to be effective this way. When its lower limbs are removed, white pine makes an excellent street tree.

## Planting and Care

White pine is easy to transplant into moist, well-drained, fertile soil but cannot tolerate heavy clays. It also needs full sun to remain fully branched to the ground, although pines growing at the southern limits of its range benefit from the afternoon shade of a taller tree. Remember that in its southernmost limits, white pine may die unexpectedly. In the foothills, mountains, and northern latitudes it does quite well.

## Different Selections

Pendula is a weeping form that is striking in the landscape when used as a specimen tree.

---

AT A GLANCE

❖

## WHITE PINE
*Pinus strobus*

**Features:** bluish needles, splendid specimen tree

**Foliage:** evergreen

**Outstanding season:** all seasons

**Height:** 50 to 80 feet

**Spread:** 20 to 40 feet

**Growth rate:** rapid

**Native:** yes

**Range:** Zones 3 to 8

**Light:** full sun

**Pests:** none specific

**Remarks:** excellent large screen tree

*Pines, such as these loblolly pines, cast a light shade and grow rapidly to provide a very tall screen.*

# Loblolly Pine

Loblolly pine may be the most familiar pine to Southern gardeners and naturalists. It is common to the native woods of the South and grows rapidly to 100 feet in the wild. In a landscape, plants will easily reach 50 feet or more. As with other pines, loblolly pines are pyramidal when young, developing a more rounded crown as they mature. The long, soft needles are about 8 inches long and grow in bundles of three. Trees have a light green cast throughout most of the year and bear cones that may remain on the tree for several years.

## In the Landscape

Fast, inexpensive, and reliable, loblolly pine should be a staple for anyone looking for quick shade around a home. Although rarely used as a single specimen, loblolly pine is a great tree for naturalizing and planting in drifts; use several at random distances along a property line to create an informal screen, taking advantage of the characteristically low branching habit of its first 15 years.

Plant a group of three to five pines as an open-lawn feature—you can easily mow beneath them when they are young; they will self-mulch when mature. If you want shade for azaleas, camellias, and ferns, no other tree will cooperate as quickly or inexpensively.

## Planting and Care

Loblolly pine prefers acid soil that is fertile, deep, and moist, but adapts to varying soil conditions. It is native to southern wetlands and is very well-suited to wet soils. It will also grow in drier soils, although not as vigorously.

## Different Selections

Fast-growing "super tree" seedlings, developed by the timber industry, are available as seedlings from some state forestry departments at a nominal cost.

AT A GLANCE
❖
### LOBLOLLY PINE
*Pinus taeda*

**Features:** yellow-green foliage; wide, flat crown
**Foliage:** evergreen
**Outstanding season:** all seasons
**Height:** 40 to 80 feet
**Spread:** 20 to 30 feet
**Growth rate:** rapid
**Native:** yes
**Range:** Zones 6 to 9
**Light:** full sun
**Pests:** none specific
**Remarks:** good fast-growing screen

# Redbud

*The blossoms of redbud pop out along the trunk and branches.*

Redbud is one of the most widely adapted native trees in the United States. It is best known for the bright magenta flowers that line the branches and even pop directly from the trunk before the leaves appear in early spring. However, anyone who plants redbud will find that long after the blooms are gone, the tree endures heat, drought, and a variety of soil types, making it one of the most versatile of all small trees.

## A Closer Look

Just as striking as the color of the blossoms is the manner in which redbud blooms. The tiny pealike flowers sprout directly from the smooth, gray bark of the stems and branches, even from the gnarly older portions of the trunk. Redbud usually flowers after the cherry trees and before the dogwoods, fading just as the dogwoods begin to bloom. The rosy-purple flower buds turn into full blooms along the branches within a week. Occasionally, blooms of different trees vary from pink to lavender or rose, but most often the trees are an unforgettable magenta. There is also an unusual white form of redbud.

The way the blooms hug the branches highlights the structure of the tree, turning it into a colorful sculpture. Immediately after the flowers, the heart-shaped leaves emerge and are reddish purple in color, quickly turning green. The leaves are 5 inches across and give the plant a coarse texture. By late spring, the branches dangle 4-inch-long, pealike pods that contain the seeds.

## In the Landscape

An easy-to-use small tree, redbud may be planted singly as the central focus of a small informal garden. The bark makes a striking silhouette in front of a stucco, brick, or wooden wall. Redbud's wide shape, coupled with its toughness in sunny spots and poor soils, makes it a good tree for shading a garden bench at the edge of a formal planting.

You may use redbud in any garden, large or small, or in an open lawn beneath shade trees. It may also be used in groupings, planted in a grove that mimics its natural growth in woods. It looks especially at home as a colorful, rustic accent planted beside a weathered outbuilding or under a gnarly pine.

---

AT A GLANCE

❖

## REDBUD
*Cercis canadensis*

**Features:** outstanding form, early magenta flowers
**Foliage:** deciduous
**Outstanding season:** spring
**Height:** 20 to 30 feet
**Spread:** 25 to 35 feet
**Growth rate:** rapid
**Native:** yes
**Range:** Zones 4 to 9
**Light:** full sun to partial shade
**Pests:** canker
**Remarks:** excellent small tree

## Planting and Care

For best growth, plant redbud in moist, well-drained soil in full sun or light shade. Trees will tolerate many soil types—acid to alkaline, sandy to clay—but they will not adapt to soggy areas. Given a good location, redbud will grow about 2 feet per year to reach a final height of 20 to 30 feet.

Redbud will reseed itself. Only very young seedlings transplant well, so dig early in the spring just as they are emerging.

## Troubleshooting

The only major pest of redbud is canker, a disease that can kill infected branches. Canker generally attacks trees weakened by poor conditions; the best protection against canker is to plant the trees in the proper location and to give them adequate water during an extended drought.

## Different Selections

Most often you will find trees labeled simply as redbud; there are few named selections. Be sure the plants you buy come from a regional source, as redbud seedlings from the North may not be adapted to the South and vice versa.

Alba is a selection with surprising white flowers; plant it with the species to create a vivid two-toned show. Forest Pansy is a handsome purple-leafed form with flowers that are slightly darker magenta than the species. The new growth on this plant is a bright reddish purple.

*Redbud is an explosion of bright color in the early spring landscape.*

*White redbud is an unusual conversation piece.*

# Sourwood

*Sourwood has some of the most graceful flowers of any tree.*

F ew native trees brighten summer with the flair of sourwood. Found on upland ridges in the wild, this slow-growing small tree also has glorious red fall color. Sourwood is a good tree for tight spaces if you are patient enough to wait for it to grow.

## A Closer Look

Sourwood is ornamental in every season. In midsummer, the soft panicles of small white flowers drape over the deep green leaves, covering the foliage like delicate strands of pearls. The tiny white flowers gently fade to form yellow seed capsules, so sourwood appears to still be blooming well into August. As the capsules mature, the foliage turns from bright green to rust red and sometimes maroon. It is one of the first to change color in late summer or fall.

Winter finds sourwood adorned with the now parchment-colored seed capsules and bright red twigs. Each tree is a unique tangle of deeply fissured bark and reddish winter twigs. Even when planted in uniform sunlight, sourwood has a wayward growth habit that lends a singular character to each tree.

## In the Landscape

Use sourwood as an accent plant at the edge of a patio or beside a sidewalk. Mimic its place in nature by planting it at the edge of a natural area or beside an expanse of lawn. The plant is not messy and therefore is a wonderful ornamental near patios and driveways. The erratic branching form and reddish overtones of both the foliage and the twigs are striking against light-colored brick walls. Use its vivid fall color as a bright contrast to yellow or orange trees.

## Planting and Care

Plant sourwood in rich, well-drained, acid soil. Full sun enhances both flowering and fall color, but it is best to plant sourwood where it is not subject to the scorching heat of midsummer. Be sure to water during periods of drought; it will drop twigs and branches in dry heat.

Sourwood is difficult to transplant. Small, container-grown seedlings have a better chance of survival than larger trees.

---

AT A GLANCE
❖
### Sourwood
*Oxydendrum arboreum*

**Features:** late summer flowers
**Foliage:** deciduous
**Outstanding season:** summer, fall
**Height:** 25 to 40 feet
**Spread:** 20 to 25 feet
**Growth rate:** slow to moderate
**Native:** yes
**Range:** Zones 4 to 8
**Light:** afternoon shade
**Pests:** none specific
**Remarks:** beautiful fall color, no named selections

*Sourwood turns bright red to maroon in fall.*

# Spruce

Norway spruce is the standard evergreen tree in the cooler parts of the country. Always distinctive, Norway spruce has a towering triangular silhouette that is highlighted by widely spreading, upswept limbs; its needle-clad branches drape like black-green fringe.

## A Closer Look

The sweeping branches give this evergreen a softer look than that of the more rigid, needle leafed, pyramidal conifers, such as Colorado spruce. Norway spruce's needles are short, stiff, and pointed, emerging a light green and then quickly changing to a dark, lustrous green. The tree bears narrow cones that are suspended from the branches.

## In the Landscape

Norway spruce and other spruces make excellent open-lawn specimens. On large lots, you may successfully plant spruce as a buffer for wind or snow, or as a privacy screen. The tree grows rapidly to 60 feet tall and spreads 25 to 30 feet wide. These graceful trees also work well when planted on either side of an entry drive on rural properties.

The foliage of Norway spruce is too long and dense to allow lawn grasses to grow. Weeds often pop up under the needle mulch left beneath the tree. A circle of landscape fabric stretched as far as the ends of the branches and covered with mulch will help prevent many weeds from sprouting.

## Planting and Care

Norway spruce prefers moist, sandy, well-drained, acid soil. Plant in full sun; in the South, it needs protection from afternoon sun.

## Different Selections

Several selections, including Pendula, Pendula Major, and Pendula Monstrosa, have draping branches that give them a graceful look.

Colorado blue spruce (*Picea pungens* Glauca) is half as tall and much more narrow than Norway spruce. It features bluish needles and stiffer branches, with a horizontal layering.

Many dwarf selections of Norway spruce are also available.

## Troubleshooting

Norway spruce may be bothered by spider mites. Turn to page 125 for more about these pests.

*Norway spruce is dependable in cool climates.*

### AT A GLANCE

❖

## SPRUCE
*Picea abies*

**Features:** pyramidal form, evergreen foliage

**Foliage:** deciduous

**Outstanding season:** all seasons

**Height:** 40 to 60 feet, can reach 100 feet

**Spread:** 25 to 30 feet

**Growth rate:** moderate to rapid

**Native:** no

**Range:** Zones 2 to 7

**Light:** full sun

**Pests:** spider mites

**Remarks:** excellent free-standing tree

# Tulip Poplar

*Although rarely seen until they fall to the ground, the tuliplike flowers of tulip poplar appear in spring.*

Tulip poplar is one of the best fast-growing shade trees you can plant. Fast-growing trees are often too brittle for landscape use; though it grows 3 to 4 feet each year, tulip poplar is strong enough to plant near your home. It is also a good shade tree, especially when planted far enough away from the house so that a falling limb would not cause damage. Eventually the tree will grow to more than 50 feet tall in the landscape, producing a high, filtered shade. In the forests of the Eastern United States, tulip poplar soars to more than 100 feet to become a hardwood giant.

## A Closer Look

Tulip poplar is named for the tulip-shaped flowers at the ends of the twigs. However, the tree does not produce flowers until it is at least 10 years old and by that time the flowering branches will be well above eye level. The yellow-green, tuliplike flowers have an orange center and are slightly fragrant; they last as long as two weeks, but because they are both hidden by the foliage and very high in the tree, you may not notice them until the petals fall to the ground.

Tulip poplar does not have a dense covering of leaves, which gives the tree a light, open canopy. The individual 8-inch leaves have a distinct blunt end, a shape unmatched by any other tree. In late summer, the apple-green leaves are the first to hint of fall, often dropping from the tree a few at a time during hot, dry weather. The tree makes a show of bright butter yellow. In the woods and along the roadside you may recognize the tree easily, as its conical crown rises above the other trees and appears to have been painted with a brush dipped in yellow.

While tulip poplar changes color early, the leaves drop slowly, gradually thinning until just a few remain high in the tree. The branching is open and sparse; the winter form is extremely upright, conical, and spare of ornamentation. The bark of older trees is gray, deeply

*The straight trunks of tulip popular bear characteristic dark, eyebrow-shaped ridges where lower limbs once hung.*

---

### AT A GLANCE

❖

### TULIP POPLAR
*Liriodendron tulipifera*

**Features:** a fast-growing shade tree

**Foliage:** deciduous

**Outstanding season:** summer

**Height:** 70 to 90 feet

**Spread:** 35 to 50 feet

**Growth rate:** fast

**Native:** yes

**Range:** Zones 4 to 9

**Light:** full sun

**Pests:** none specific

**Remarks:** may be brittle

furrowed, and ridged with fissures sometimes as deep as ½ inch. Winter also reveals the upright seed capsules at the ends of the branches; these look like dried flowers.

## In the Landscape

Tulip poplar is a large tree that requires a large area for the roots to feed. Avoid planting it closer than 15 feet from paved surfaces; the root system may crack or heave the surface, and the tree will suffer in a small feeding area.

Use tulip poplar as a feature tree in an expanse of open lawn or in a grouping of three trees within a natural area in the lawn. This tree is a superb choice for a fast-growing shade tree. For shade during the hottest part of the day, plant it on the west or southwest side of your house, at least 40 feet from the building, in an area of rich soil.

## Planting and Care

Tulip poplar prefers full sun and moist, well-drained soil that is loamy; a natural area where you allow the leaves to decay is most like its habitat in the wild. This tree does not do well in sandy, arid locations.

The tree will signal drought stress by a premature yellowing and dropping of its leaves. Immediate and thorough watering may help; you must keep tulip poplar watered during dry weather.

## Different Selections

There are few named selections available. Arnold is a compact form that is more narrow than the species.

*Tulip poplar turns a buttery yellow in the fall.*

119

# Valuable Native Trees

*Native hickories blaze in autumn.*

You may find that you have one or more of these four native trees—shagbark hickory (or other hickories), sycamore, red cedar, or sassafras—already growing on your property. These are valuable trees that are not always available at nurseries but are often found on undeveloped lots. Here is a quick look at what they offer and why you may wish to keep them.

## Planting and Care

You will probably not be planting most of these trees because they are seldom available at garden centers. However, you may dig up and transplant very young seedlings from one place to another on your property. Transplant in winter; select a young tree that is only a foot tall. Dig it with a long-bladed drain spade, leaving a ball of soil around the roots so as not to disturb them; this is especially critical with hickory and sassafras, which have a long tap root and resent transplanting. (Sycamore and red cedar are easier to find in nurseries than hickories and sassafras because they do not have a tap root.)

Plant all of these trees in full sun.

## Hickory

Shagbark hickory is the most easily recognized hickory because of its novel bark. The dark gray bark on the columnar trunk appears to be splitting off in strips that curl outward at the ends. This bark is so conspicuous that immediate identification is certain; fallen hickory nuts will also confirm the tree's identity.

Make a place for this hardwood tree for its gorgeous fall color. The tree is durable and the foliage is of an unmatchable quality.

## A Closer Look

Shagbark hickory grows at a slow to moderate rate to reach a mature height of 60 to 80 feet. It develops a narrow, oblong crown, with the lower branches pointing to the ground and the upper branches ascending. The deep yellow-green leaves are compound, having five 4- to 6-inch-long leaflets on each stem.

## In the Landscape

If you already have a hickory, plant dogwood or sourwood nearby. Both are companions of hickory in the wild, so the combination will naturalize well. Consider underplanting hickory with ground cover or mulch so that the nuts will fall into an area that will not be mowed.

---

### AT A GLANCE
❖
### SHAGBARK HICKORY
*Carya ovata*

**Features:** excellent fall color, handsome bark

**Foliage:** deciduous

**Outstanding season:** fall

**Height:** 60 to 80 feet

**Spread:** 30 to 40 feet

**Growth rate:** moderate to slow

**Native:** yes

**Range:** Zones 4 to 9

**Light:** full sun

**Pests:** none specific

**Remarks:** great fall backdrop in natural areas

## Different Selections

The yellow fall color, falling nuts, and characteristic leaves will help you identify other hickories, such as shellbark hickory (*Carya laciniosa*), pignut hickory (*Carya glabra*), and bitternut hickory (*Carya cordiformis*).

## Red Cedar

Red cedar may seem too common for garden use, yet these long-lived, tough trees transform into hardy beauties. This deeply colored evergreen, which grows at a medium rate to 60 feet tall with an 8- to 20-foot spread, is ironclad in both hardiness and adaptability to severe environmental conditions, such as the salt and sand of the beach.

## A Closer Look

While young red cedars are indistinguishable from one another, older trees vary from narrow and columnar to densely pyramidal, even slightly weeping habits of growth. The individual leaves cloak the tree so thickly that the brown woody branches are rarely visible until the tree is older. The foliage is medium green in summer, becoming a dark black green in winter. Some trees have a maroon cast in cold weather.

The bark is a light, rich reddish brown that peels in strips. As the tree ages, the trunk becomes twisted and strongly corded, an effect that is enhanced by the peeling bark.

Older trees will bloom inconspicuously and then produce powder blue berries. The combination of fruit and thick foliage make red cedar an attractive nesting site for birds.

## In the Landscape

On open properties or at the beach, plant rows of trees as a living windbreak. You may use the tree formally, in rows or in pairs along a sidewalk. Red cedar is often seeded by birds.

## Planting and Care

Plant red cedar in full sun and well-drained soil, either acid or alkaline. It grows well in sand or clay.

## Troubleshooting

Red cedar may be bothered by bagworms. See caterpillars, pages 124–125, for more about bagworms.

*Environmental stresses, such as salt-laden breezes or prevailing winds, impart a muscular character to red cedar.*

**AT A GLANCE**
❖
## RED CEDAR
*Juniperus virginiana*

**Features:** reddish bark
**Foliage:** evergreen
**Outstanding season:** all seasons
**Height:** 40 to 50 feet
**Spread:** 8 to 20 feet
**Growth rate:** medium
**Native:** yes
**Range:** Zones 2 to 9
**Light:** full sun
**Pests:** bagworms
**Remarks:** salt and drought tolerant

*In fall, sassafras turns an array of colors, including this vivid scarlet.*

# Sassafras

Sassafras often grows in colonies along a woodland edge in poor, rocky soil. Planted as a solitary specimen, it becomes a showy, medium-sized shade tree. In spring, the tree produces light green flowers, but autumn alone is reason to grow sassafras.

## A Closer Look

The foliage is bright to medium green in summer but becomes splendidly vivid in fall, racing through yellow, lingering in orange, and then becoming scarlet and even purple. The corky, reddish-brown, deeply ridged bark provides subtle winter landscape effect. In spring, pale yellow flowers hang from the tips of the leafless branches. The flowers mature into dark blue fruits that ripen in September and are quickly eaten by birds.

Sassafras sports three types of leaves: mitten shaped, single lobed, or three lobed. This makes identification easy.

## Planting and Care

Seedlings often volunteer, especially on sites disturbed by construction. You may want to choose a few to keep and clear the rest to allow enough room for the selected ones to grow to their final size: 30 to 60 feet high and 25 feet or more in width.

## Troubleshooting

Sassafras is often bothered by Japanese beetles. Turn to beetles on page 124 to read more about these pests.

*The yellow flowers of sassafras decorate the ends of the twigs before the leaves emerge.*

---

### AT A GLANCE

❖

### SASSAFRAS
*Sassafras albidum*

**Features:** pale yellow flowers, orange fall color

**Foliage:** deciduous

**Outstanding season:** fall

**Height:** 30 to 60 feet

**Spread:** 25 to 40 feet

**Growth rate:** medium

**Native:** yes

**Range:** Zones 4 to 8

**Light:** full sun

**Pests:** Japanese beetles

**Remarks:** tolerates poor soil

# Sycamore

Sycamore, also known as American plane tree, grows naturally in wet soils, such as the bottom of a creek or a river basin, but is also well adapted to dry areas. It grows rapidly, reaching massive stature with a height of 75 to 100 feet and a canopy of large, light green leaves. It is a landscape showstopper that requires a lot of space but justifies every square foot in winter, when its white bark is beautifully silhouetted against a blue sky.

## A Closer Look

The white-and-cream bark of the upper branches and trunk is sycamore's hallmark and the key to identification. Low on the trunk, the bark is reddish brown and slightly scaly. This covering peels away to reveal the white underbark that is gorgeous against winter's skies.

The leaves are similar in shape to maple leaves and may be 10 inches wide. Inconspicuous flowers are followed by pendulous fruit, roughened balls about the size of sweet-gum balls, but not as numerous or durable.

## In the Landscape

Sycamore balls, as the fruit is called, are a nuisance, so keep this tree away from areas where you walk, sit, or park your car. The large leaves are somewhat difficult to rake; plant the tree in a natural area where raking is not necessary.

Sycamore is too large to be a street tree. Plant it as a specimen or as the anchor tree in a distant garden corner. Due to its vigorous root system, you should avoid planting it near a septic drain field.

## Planting and Care

Plant sycamore in full sun. It grows well in sand or clay and will tolerate wet locations. Sycamore will grow in acid or alkaline soil.

## Troubleshooting

This tree is subject to anthracnose, a fungal infection that delays the production of leaves. London plane tree *(Platanus x acerifolia)*, a hybrid selection, is also subject to anthracnose. A close relative to sycamore, Oriental plane tree *(Platanus orientalis)* is immune.

Trees may also be attacked by lacebugs. See page 125 for more about lacebugs.

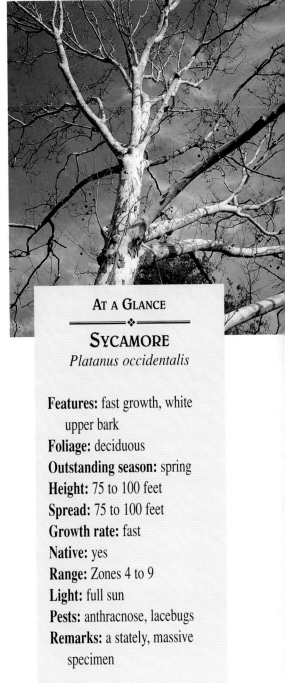

*In winter, the mottled and whitened upper branches of sycamore are starkly beautiful against the clear blue sky.*

---

**AT A GLANCE**

❖

## SYCAMORE
*Platanus occidentalis*

**Features:** fast growth, white upper bark

**Foliage:** deciduous

**Outstanding season:** spring

**Height:** 75 to 100 feet

**Spread:** 75 to 100 feet

**Growth rate:** fast

**Native:** yes

**Range:** Zones 4 to 9

**Light:** full sun

**Pests:** anthracnose, lacebugs

**Remarks:** a stately, massive specimen

# Pests and Diseases

The following insects and diseases are common pests of the trees in this book. Insects and diseases are most damaging to a tree that is already weakened by poor growing conditions or other means, so remember that the best form of control is to maintain the overall health of the tree. Timing is also very important to controlling insects, as you must kill the first generation before they are able to reproduce and cause more damage.

Many pesticides are available to help you fight pests, but the recommendations for using these products frequently change. Try mild pesticides, such as insecticidal soap, before using stronger substances. Always use pesticides strictly according to label directions. For information about specific pesticides, please contact your local Extension office, which is listed under the county Department of Agriculture in your blue pages.

## Aphids

Aphids are tiny, pear-shaped insects that are about ⅛ to ¼ inch long; they are frequently green or black but may also be yellow or pink. They harm trees by sucking sap from the tender young leaves, stems, and buds, causing growth to be distorted and preventing the buds from opening. Crape myrtle and river birch are two of their favorite trees, although they will also feed on many other species.

Aphids are worst in spring and fall. They will produce hundreds of offspring in a few weeks, so it is crucial to control them as soon as they appear. They often disappear on their own once the temperature reaches 90 degrees.

Sooty mold, a black fungus, may grow on the aphid secretions left on the tree. This condition, while not attractive, will not damage the tree and will disappear once the aphids are controlled.

## Beetles

Beetles are hard-bodied insects that chew on the leaves and tender stems of trees. While most fly in and out of the tree and feed without noticeable damage, they occasionally reach outlandish numbers and will strip a tree of its leaves. There are many kinds of beetles that damage trees; among them are Japanese beetles, which love sassafras, flowering peach, and cherry trees but will feed on anything green.

Beetles are very difficult to control once they begin to be a problem. They usually feed in hordes, with hundreds present at one time. Dusting foliage with a recommended pesticide helps, but you must keep the dust on new growth as it unfurls. The best way to control Japanese beetles is to kill the larvae, called *grubs,* which feed in the lawn. To do this most effectively, join forces with your neighbors, who are no doubt being affected by this pest as well, in order to treat a large area.

## Borers

Borers, the larvae of moths or beetles, tunnel through tree trunks and branches. Almost any tree may fall victim to borers, but the most likely to be attacked are cherry, dogwood, and pine. Borers are especially damaging to young trees and those already weakened by prolonged drought or construction damage. Trees attacked by borers require professional attention. Tree-care professionals have the proper equipment to spray high up in the canopy of a tree, and they are licensed to apply restricted insecticides.

## Caterpillars

Caterpillars are the larvae of moths and butterflies. They generally feed on a tree's leaves without your knowledge and without causing any serious damage;